Wounded in the House of a Friend

Howard Ryan

What Others Are Saying

About CEM

Here are some excerpts from letters of reference from denominational leaders & pastors from across the country.

> I just wanted to drop this note to you and say a personal thank you for the work you have done in providing administrative management, counseling perspective, and pastoral oversight for the people during these past months. It has been one of the more difficult assignments that could have been given to anyone. May the Lord provide all the resources necessary to maintain spiritual equilibrium and Godly vision for the days ahead.

> *Rev. T. Ray Rachel, A District Superintendent*
> *Southern California*

> It was my joy and pleasure to have had Brother Ryan in our recent minister's institute as one of our speakers. His ministry was of great value to the ministers of our District. I would recommend his ministry to any District, and I am sure that you would find his ministry a blessing to the Pastors, Ministers Institutes and Retreats, as well to the churches of your district.

> *Rev. Howard V. Spruill, Former District Superintendent*
> *Maryland*

> This letter comes to you in appreciation for the fine way that you presented the materials at our Church Growth Seminar in Concord, California. Many verbal reports have been received expressing how much our ministers and church leaders were helped by your ministry. We are pleased to recommend you to all.

> *Rev. R. L. Hardcastle, Former Secretary/Treasurer*
> *Northern California*
> *Northern California District*

"The District Executive expresses to Dr. Howard Ryan appreciation from the churches of Manitoba and Northwestern Ontario for his timely and helpful ministry."

We want to express to Dr. Ryan our appreciation for doing an outstanding job and going beyond the call of duty. Thanks to your leadership, we believe the future is bright, and we are now able to concentrate on the purpose of winning the lost.

Rev. Vernon W. Taylor, Former District Superintendent, Canada, Manitoba/Western Ontario

You are a blessing to our entire fellowship. You help pastors and boards zero in on their purpose and build bridges of communication.

Kentucky District Presbytery

I am writing to say how much you were appreciated by our constituency and how meaningful your contribution was to our convention. I am most grateful for your generous help in making our time together both pleasant and spiritually beneficial. Do not be too surprised if you should hear from us again, "Come over and help us".

Rev. Errol K. Alchin, President Canada

What Others Are Saying

From Pastors

"I have known Howard for many years and have always appreciated his fine ministry. Recently we had him at Faith Chapel for a "*Church Enrichment Seminar*". Our church greatly benefited from his fine presentation of the Word. I highly commend him to you. Your people will be helped and blessed."

Rev. George Gregg, Former Pastor of Faith Chapel, La Mesa, CA. (now deceased, Southern CA.)

"Once again", thank you for the day you spent with us here at our church. At the close of the Sunday evening service, with the altars full, and lives being changed...I knew that we had experienced more than just a time of sharing, we had camp meeting.

With all consulted, you were the speaker of preference for our up-coming couples retreat. I will contact you later as to the exact dates."

Rev. Alton Garrison
Assistant General Superintendent., Springfield, Missouri

Aside from the fact that I feel rather badly about your leaving First Assembly, Chula Vista, and your leaving us as a leader of our area churches, I do confess a measure of excitement about the prospects that are before you. I have been very pleased with the leadership you have given us - and on that basis, see no reason why you cannot serve most effectively in this greater area of responsibility.

Rev. Richard Dresselhaus, Executive Presbyter
Southern California

"I have known and worked with Howard Ryan since 1956. It is my opinion that Howard has one of the most needed ministries for the body of Christ today. He is a man of the highest integrity, who has a consuming desire to enrich the pastor and to build up the body of Christ. I commend him to you, and give him my highest recommendation without reservation."

Dr. David A. Lewis
Evangelist, Teacher, In Prophecy & Related Subjects
Springfield, Missouri

"I do not personally know of anyone who has more to offer for church enrichment in the ministry of assistance, helps, and administration than Howard. In addition, his "Family Enrichment Seminars" are indeed rich…."

Rev. Colman McDuff, CA
Southern California

What a great week of inspiration, brain-storming, and helpful suggestions! I personally benefited from your ministry as well as the members of our staff. When we digest what you have given, we will be inviting you back.

Rev. Ron Prinzing, Pastor
Southern California

I can whole-heartedly recommend Church Enrichment Ministries and Rev. H.S. Ryan, to any church that has a vision for higher quality and growth. The sessions with the church and ministerial staff, church board, and office employees made the seminar worthwhile, not to speak of the personal sessions which added greatly to my ministry as Senior Pastor.

Rev. Don Young
Longtime friend & Sr. Pastor, Southern California

The purpose of this letter is to give you my personal appraisal of Dr. Ryan's' ministry. Both the Church/Family Enrichment Seminars, in my opinion, deal with some of the greatest challenges facing our pastors and congregations today. Through all the services, there were only favorable comments. I heartily recommend Brother Ryan's ministry to you."

Rev. Vincent Beemer, Former Pastor
Manassas, VA

What Others Are Still Saying

If you are pastoring a growing church and are in need of the ministry of helps and administrations, I trust that you will seriously consider inviting Dr. Ryan to share with you. I personally believe that God has raised up his ministry for such a time as this.

Rev. Robert Wise, District Superintendent
Southern New England

I am writing this letter to recommend the ministry of Howard Ryan. Dr. Ryan has been a tremendous blessing to the church that I pastored, and to me personally. In the past and for several years Brother Ryan has conducted a Pastor/board/ Staff Retreat for us. The benefit has been overwhelming. His anointed teaching, mixed with his keen sense of humor, has proven to be the perfect ingredients for a revival in the leadership of this church.

To adequately describe all the benefits derived from my association with brother Ryan, would take more time and space than anyone might appreciate, so I will simply say, it would be hard for me to imagine a pastor, church, church board, or staff who would not benefit from his ministry.

Rev. Garold Finch, Former Senior Pastor in Kentucky

Words cannot begin to express how pleased I was with the ministry of Rev. Howard Ryan as he spoke for us while pastoring in Kentucky. As well as at my Pastor/Staff/Board Retreat that I previously held at the same church.

Now involved in district leadership, I still appreciate his sensitivity to have spoken what God had laid on his heart. At the close of a most precious meeting, it culminated in the altars being filled and many people openly weeping in the presence of the Lord for a greater move of God in their lives, and in our church.

Brother Ryan has proven to be a most discerning and sensitive man of God. Without my speaking to him at all prior to our retreat, many of the issues he shared focused directly on the areas of leadership that our board and staff needed to hear. I am confident that you could not go wrong if you are looking for a consultant or motivational encourager for your church or church leaders.

Rev. Joseph Girdler, District Leadership, Kentucky

Thank you for being with us for our Christian Winter Conference. Your ministry to the 180 couples on the subject "Marriage Can Be Fun" was greatly enjoyed and many marriages were healed.

We want you to be back to us again when you are ready with your next series, "The Power of Communication". Or "What you heard is not what I said." We love and appreciate you both very much, and are thankful for your ministry at Willow Valley.

Rev. John Hamercheck (now deceased)
Evangelist, and Director
Christian Winter Retreats, Willow Valley Retreat Center, Lancaster,
PA

Always Remember

"Nothing Ever Takes God By Surprise"

Wounded in the House of a Friend

Howard Ryan

Copyright 2015©Howard Ryan

ISBN 978-1-61529-157-1

Vision Publishing
1672 Main St. E109
Ramona, CA 92065
www.booksbyvision.com
1 800 9 VISION
All rights reserved worldwide.

Table of Contents

Foreword

It is my pleasure to recommend the teachings of Dr. Howard Ryan. Throughout his life, Dr. Ryan ministered to broken people helping them gain new life and strength to meet the challenges of the day. He did this with humor. But the humor had content. It was my privilege to sit with him and regularly discuss the serious matters of conflict in community and biblical patterns that would help us function in a healthy way. I watched him take assignments of pastoring churches that were broken and turn them into places of refuge for the lost and dying. I miss my friend and look forward to meeting him again in heaven. I encourage you to let him speak to you through this book, "Wounded In the House of A Friend."

Terry Wiles, Bishop

"Wounded in the House of a Friend"

"**And** one will say to him, 'What are these wounds between your arms? Then he will answer, 'Those with which I was wounded in the house of my friends." Zechariah13:6 NKJV

Introduction

It is a sad commentary on the church today, that so many, perhaps even some that you once knew, who have enjoyed the born again experience and were involved in the ministries of their church that went on to be spiritually wounded by the unsavory words or carnal attitude of someone in leadership. If so, they may be among those who have become listed among the missing in action (MIA's). As a result, they may no longer be attending an Evangelical Church anywhere. It is almost unthinkable that so many believers have been wounded by unkind words or the wrong attitude of someone professing to be a Christian, one who has hypocritically lead the church and represented the cause of Christ to a point of shame.

Just a thought:

Anyone who professes to be a Christian will no doubt face persecution and daily challenges. Church members and their constituents need to consider the effect of "conflict" on each individual's life. The following is something I have brought to the attention of churches in which I have ministered, and also to minister's meetings where I have had the privilege of sharing the grief of those who were unexpectedly caught in a church conflict.

In everyday life, there are those who attend college, have families, go to work, and in many cases attend church for spiritual strength and encouragement. In most cases, they seem to be able to deal with problems that affect them during their college years, unless they are facing what appears to be insurmountable; then they often cannot find peace and solace at their preferred place of worship. This conflict affects their home and family.

If they are facing problems at home as well, then church conflicts can be seen as even more difficult to deal with. These conflicts can also affect their job and its ancillary areas of responsibility, especially when there are difficulties on the job. Then if the same difficulties are happening at the church, their vulnerability to disappointment and discouragement may disrupt their faith.

The following are the words written by the Apostle Paul to the church at Corinth about the attitude of some that would not repent of the conflicts. It is from this passage that the title for this work is derived.

2 Corinthians 12:14-21 (special emphasis added by author)

14 Now I am ready to visit you for the third time, and I will not be a burden to you, because what I want is not your possessions BUT YOU. 15 After all, children should not have to save up for their parents, but parents for their children. 16 So I will very gladly spend for you everything I have and expend myself as well. 17 If I love you more, will you love me less? 18 Be that as it may, I have not been a burden to you. Yet, crafty fellow that I am, I caught you by trickery! Did I exploit you through any of the men I sent you? 19 I urged Titus to go to you and I sent our brother with him. Titus did not exploit you, did he? Did we not act in the same spirit and follow the same course? 20 Have you been thinking all along that we have been defending ourselves to you? We have been speaking in the sight of God as those in Christ; and everything we do, dear friends, is for your strengthening. I am afraid that when I come I may not find you as I want you to be, and you may not find me as you want me to be. 21 I fear that there may be:

- Quarreling,
- Jealousy,
- Outbursts Of Anger,
- Factions,
- Slander,
- Gossip,
- Arrogance and
- Disorder.

I am afraid that when I come again my God will humble me before you, and I will be grieved over many who have sinned earlier and have not repented of, sexual sin and debauchery in which they have indulged.

Paul loved this church, and wanted them to move to maturity. Their conflict made it nearly impossible to fulfill their kingdom mandate, and sadly, similar problems to the church in Corinth continue today, and have become the passion of this author's heart.

Having been invited since the year 1980, to deal, with the administrative responsibilities of working 42 churches, with some having disagreements that have all too often occurred in churches, among not only within church boards, but in business meetings, as well as various committees and even individual members of families. It was during this time that I realized that many uninvolved and unrelated to the problems existing in any given church were being "wounded in action," due to things that were openly said and done during times of church malfunctions, resulting in my forming a humble opinion that there are many, former church members and constituents who no longer attend any church due to their having to endure an unexpected church conflict, or even worse, that in some cases could even be considered an unnecessary tragedy. All too often this has resulted in total confusion, especially to the new or at least recent converts.

Then there are the suggestions of the evil one himself, the devil, convincing them that there is no one they can really trust in or out of the church. Due to continued discouragement, and loss of confidence, especially in the ones they trusted, they no longer seek His direction. They just give up in frustration and stop going to any church anywhere. Our adversary loves confusion within the body of Christ. In His final prayer before His crucifixion, recorded in John 17, Jesus prayed for His followers that UNITY would be accomplished for all who followed Him.

Then added to the existing problems of half-truths and innuendos, the constant phone calls that may include both some truth and indeed, some gossip filled errors that have many times had a disastrous effect on those that might not have even been involved or understood what the problem is all about. This then has more times than not, become a completely debilitating, and sometimes unbearable area of challenge, especially for those who have innocently become involved.

If and when any of those situations occur, especially when particularly vulnerable members and friends are facing other tests and trials, the church becomes involved in conflict. It may be responsible, causing a loss of faith and trust in leadership. As a result, our adversary may endeavor to replace their faith with confusion, and could affect or even infect, the entire church family.

I believe it would be profitable to His Kingdom, for any who profess to be a child of God, to seriously consider, not only this next verse, but the ones that follow. The practice of obedience could be, and would be, another step toward maturity.

> James 1:26 KJV If any man among you seem to be religious, and bridleth not his tongue, but deceiveth his own heart, this man's religion is vain.

> James 3:5-9 KJV Even so the tongue is a little member, and boasteth great things. Behold, how great a matter a little fire kindled! 6 And the tongue is a fire, a world of iniquity: so is the tongue among our members, that it defiles the whole body, and setteth on fire the course of nature; and it is set on fire of hell. 7 For every kind of beasts, and of birds, and of serpents, and of things in the sea, is tamed, and hath been tamed of mankind: 8 But the tongue can no man tame; it is an unruly evil, full of deadly poison. 9 Therewith bless we God, even the Father; and therewith curse we men, which are made after the similitude of God.

Might there be a former convert, who may have started attending and then possibly have become a member of an evangelical church and labored in the vineyard of his kingdom, that are now listed as M.I.A.? They may have been forgotten by most due to new recruits that take their place. They seem to no longer be needed or even be remembered by other church members who are still attending and busily working in the ministries offered by their church.

Are there challenges for control in churches today? While the call of Jesus has always been for unity, is it possible that a personal agenda may include a challenge for leadership that might not only be invisible, but is, at times ,openly identified in the business or board meeting? This is often the case, especially when there is an absence of unity among individual leaders.

It is even conceivable that during these attacks on Christianity, especially from outside the church walls, that there may be those as described by the Apostle Paul in 1 Cor. 12 as carnal. Their desire is to see their own personal agendas fulfilled, having their minds made up, regardless of the cost of divisiveness. They are set on having their own way, and may be unjustly planning to replace those in positions of leadership to fulfill, under the guise of concern for the church, their own carnal reasoning.

In the early church, according to the book of Acts, the qualifications of the ones first chosen for leadership were:

> Acts 6:2-7 KJV Then the twelve called the multitude of the disciples unto them, and said, it is not reason that we should leave the word of God, and serve tables. 3 Wherefore, brethren, look ye out among you seven men of honest report, full of the Holy Ghost and wisdom, whom we may appoint over this business. 4 But we will give ourselves continually to prayer, and to the ministry of the word. 5 And the saying pleased the whole multitude: and they chose Stephen, a man full of faith and of the Holy Ghost, and Philip, and Prochorus, and Nicanor, and Timon, and Parmenas, and Nicolas a proselyte of Antioch: 6 Whom they set before the apostles and when they prayed, they lay their hands on them. 7 And the word of God increased; and the number of the disciples multiplied in Jerusalem greatly; and a great company of the priests were obedient to the faith.

This book endeavors to point out the common, as well as the individual frailties and failures of the human spirit. Self-serving carnal attitudes may endeavor to invade and control the direction of some growing churches, or even some apparently successful para-church ministries. Many of these have been affected to some point, and some have even become "infected." This happens in spite of the fact that they may have been among some of the most fundamentally, as well as spiritually sound, organizations!

Listen carefully to the following warnings from Jesus himself and the early church fathers, including the apostle Paul, regarding inappropriate attitudes.

> Matt 7:15-16 NIV "Watch out for false prophets". They come to you in sheep's clothing, but inwardly they are ferocious wolves. 16 by their fruit you will recognize them. Do people pick grapes from thorn bushes, or figs from thistles?

> Acts 20:29-31 KJV for I know this, that after my departing shall grievous wolves enter in among you, not sparing the flock. 30 also of your own selves shall men arise, speaking perverse things, to draw away disciples after them. 31 Therefore, watch and remember that by the space of three years I ceased not to warn every one night and day with tears.

Warnings Against False Prophets

We have here a caution against false prophets. Take heed that we be not deceived and imposed upon by them. Prophets are to foretell things to come; there are some mentioned in the Old Testament who pretended to do that without warrant, and the event disproved their pretensions. For an example, look at Zedekiah in 1 Kings 22:11, and another Zedekiah in Jeremiah 29:21.

But prophets were also to teach the people their duty, so that false prophets are also false teachers. Christ was a Prophet and a Teacher who came from God; he desired to send teachers under him abroad. He gives a warning to all to take heed of the counterfeits, (fake, phony, imitation) that, instead of healing souls with wholesome doctrine, would poison them.

They are false teachers and false prophets who produce false commissions. They pretend to have an immediate warrant and direction from God as prophets. They claim to be divinely inspired, when they are not. Though their doctrine may be true, we are to beware of them as false prophets. False apostles are those who say they are apostles, and are not (Rev 2:2). "Take heed of those who pretend to revelation, and admit them not without sufficient proof, lest that one absurdity being admitted, a thousand follow."

Those who teach that which is contrary to the truth as it is in Jesus, are pseudo-prophets. A false prophet would hang out false colors, but with design and under pretense, more successfully attack the truth.

> "Well, beware of them, suspect them, try them, and when you have discovered their falsehood, avoid them, have nothing to do with them. Stand upon your guard against this temptation, which commonly attends the days of reformation, and the breakings out of divine light in more than ordinary strength and splendor." [1]

When God's work is revived, Satan and his agents are most busy. We need to be very cautious, because their pretenses are fair and plausible, and as such can deceive us, if we are not on our guard.

> Zech 13:4 They come in sheep's clothing, in the habit of prophets, which was plain and coarse, and unwrought; they wear a rough garment to deceive.

> Luke 20:46 Elijah's mantle the Septuagint calls the melote - a sheepskin mantle. We must take heed of being imposed upon by men's dress and garb, as by that of the scribes, who desire to walk in long robes.

> In 2 Corinthians 11:13-14 it may be taken figuratively; they pretend to be sheep, and outwardly appear innocent, harmless, meek, useful, and all that is good, as to be excelled by none; they feign themselves to be just men, and for the sake of their clothing are admitted among the sheep, which gives them an opportunity to do mischief ere they are aware. They and their errors are gilded with special pretenses of sanctity and devotion. Satan turns himself into an angel of light, the enemy has horns like a lamb (Rev 13:11); faces

---

[1] Source of quote lost

of men, Rev 9:7-8, seducers in language and carriage are soft as wool, Rom 16:18; Isa 30:10.

John 10:12 Because under these pretensions their designs are very malicious and mischievous; inwardly they are ravening wolves. A hypocrite is a goat in sheep's clothing; not only not a sheep, but the worst enemy the sheep has, that comes to tear and devour, to scatter the sheep, to drive them from God, and from one another, into crooked paths.

Here is a good rule to go by.

We must prove all things (1 Thessalonians 5:21), try the spirits (1 John 4:1), and here we have a touchstone; ye shall know them by their fruits, 16-20.

Please observe;

The illustration for comparison is of the fruit identifying the tree. You cannot always distinguish the tree by their bark and leaves, nor by the spreading of their boughs, but by their fruits ye shall know them. The fruit is according to the tree. Men may, in their professions, put a force upon their nature, and contradict their inward principles, but the stream and bent of their practices will agree with them. Christ insists upon this, the agreeableness between the fruit and the tree, which is such as that.

If you know what the tree is, you may know what fruit to expect. Never look to gather grapes from thorns, nor figs from thistles; it is not in their nature to produce such fruits. An apple

may be stuck, or a bunch of grapes may hang, upon a thorn; so may a good truth, a good word or action, be found in a bad man, but you may be sure it never grew there.

Please Note;

1. Corrupt, vicious, unsanctified hearts are like thorns and thistles, which came in with sin. They will, in the end, be thrown into the fire.

2. Good works are good fruit, like grapes and figs, pleasing to God and profitable to men.

3. This good fruit is never to be expected from bad men, and more than a clean thing out of an unclean: they want an influencing acceptable principle. Evil treasure will bring forth evil things.

Matt 3:7-10 NIV

> 7 But when he saw many of the Pharisees and Sadducees coming to where he was baptizing, he said to them: "You brood of vipers! Who warned you to flee from the coming wrath"? 8 Produce fruit in keeping with repentance. 9 And do not think you can say to yourselves, 'We have Abraham as our father.' I tell you that out of these stones God can raise up children for Abraham. 10 The ax is already at the root of the trees, and every tree that does not produce good fruit will be cut down and thrown into the fire. Christ could have spoken the same sense in other words; could have altered it, or given it a new turn; but he thought it no disparagement to him to say the same that John had said before him; let not ministers be ambitious of coining new expressions, nor people's ears itch for novelties; to write and speak the same things must not be grievous, for it is safe.

The description of barren trees shows that trees that do not bring forth good fruit; though there be fruit, if it is not good fruit, the tree is considered barren. The doom of barren trees is that they shall be hewn down and cast into the fire. God will deal with them as men use to deal with dry trees that encumber the ground: he will mark them by signal tokens of his displeasure, he will bark them by stripping them of their parts and gifts, and will cut them down by death, and cast them into the fire of hell, a fire blown with the bellows of God's wrath, and fed with the wood of barren trees. Compare this with Ezekiel 31:12-13; Dan 4:14; John 15:6.

By the fruits of their person, their words and actions, and the course of their conversation, you shall know them. If you want to know whether they are right or not, observe how they live; their work will testify for them or against them. The scribes and the Pharisees sat in the chair of Moses and taught the law; but they were proud, covetous, false, and oppressive. Therefore Christ warned his disciples to beware of them and of their leaven, Mark 12:38. If men pretend to be prophets and are immoral, that disproves their pretensions; they are not true friends of the cross of Christ. God puts his treasure into earthen vessels, but not into such corrupt vessels. They may declare God's statutes, but what have they to do to declare them?

By the fruit of their doctrine; their fruit as prophets: one can judge if they are from God. It is one way of trying doctrines, whether they are of God or not. What do they tend to do? What affections and practices will their doctrines lead them into that embrace them?

If the doctrine is from God, it will promote piety, humility, charity, holiness, and love; along with other Christian graces. If, on the contrary, the doctrines these prophets preach have a manifest tendency to make people proud, worldly, and contentious, to make them loose and careless in their conversations, unjust or uncharitable, factious or disturbers of the public peace; if it encourages carnal liberty, and takes people away from governing themselves and their families by the strict rules of the narrow way, we may conclude that this persuasion comes not of him that calleth us, Gal 5:8. This wisdom is from above, James 3:15. Faith and a good conscience are held together, 1 Tim 1:19; 3:9.

Note: Doctrines of doubtful disputation must be tried by the graces and duties of confessed certainty. Those opinions come not from God that lead to sin, but if we cannot know them by their fruits, we must have recourse to the great touchstone, to the law, and to the testimony. Do they speak according to that rule?[2]

---

[2]   Comment Quotes are from Matthew Henry's *Commentary on the Whole Bible*.

The Sordid History
of Conflict in the Church

How long has the church been involved in conflict and plagued by those who professed to be religious? The answer is, since the beginning of the Church (Acts 2,) it is known as the Body of Christ.

The fact is, conflict in church did not start with your church, nor will it end with it.

As long as human attitudes and personal agendas persist, conflict will continue. It has since the church began in Jerusalem 2000 years ago. Bad attitudes come with the unsanctified professors of Christianity. It gives them opportunity to make examples out of the failures. The world, individually as well as collectively (media), blames this on all professing to be a Christian and holding all of Christianity in contempt.

We hear a lot about the following terms in connection with Christianity and the person of Jesus Christ, the Son of God. Just how do you think that they apply?

Which one of the following positions do you believe Jesus, as the Son of God, most fulfilled?

Conservative	[ ]
Moderate	[ ]
Liberal	[ ]
Legalist	[ ]

Shouldn't He still expect faithfulness from His followers?

How did Jesus address those with whom He came in contact?

- Demons and evil, he always addressed with authority
- The world, he addressed with authenticity

- Those of his followers, he sometimes addressed with a stern defense of his Father's will!

In my mind, there are at least 3 areas of potential weakness in the Christian Church. They are: Familiarity breeds contempt, Spiritual fatigue, and Apathy.

That is, a specific time where repentance can take place and a change in attitudes (or fruit of the Spirit) can be readily recognized.

The following is a list of the names of individuals from whose life styles and attitudes we might learn to discern the affect our attitudes may have on the gospel, for both good and evil.

Especially by those who did damage to the gospel, ask yourself this question. Do the spirit and/or attitude of any of these people who were involved in the early church attend the same church you now attend or now pastor, or have pastored?

Demos (hath departed to Thessalonica, having loved this present world more than the things of God.)	Ananias and Sapphira (lied to the Holy Spirit) Died on the spot for the sin of lying to the Holy Spirit!
Alexander (had a bad spirit)	Hymenaeus, Alexander, and Philetus
Bar-jesus: (Elymas the sorcerer)	Simon the Sorcerer
Diotrephes (a misfit and disappointment in church leadership)	The Slave Girl (An evil spirit by which she told the future)
JUDAS	Judas, a betrayer of truth with a kiss

Alexander the metal worker.	Did me a great deal of harm. The Lord will repay him for what he has done
Are you blessed,	By the attitudes of those on the following list?
Euodias & Syntyche, Phil 4:1-3	dedicated workers, but at odds with each other
Paul & Barnabas	Untiring love and devotion to their savior
Peter	Matt 16:23 because he was a man of deep feelings, it became one possible explanation for his denial.
Tabitha	The results of a living faith
Cornelius	A man, well loved & respected
Demetrius	Well-spoken of by everyone
Epaphroditus	Phil.2:25 a man of sacrifice
Gaius	A letter to a friend from the Apostle John

Acts 5:3-8

3 Peter said, "Ananias, how is it that Satan has so filled your heart that you have lied to the Holy Spirit and have kept for yourself some of the money you received for the land? 4 Didn't it belong to you before it was sold? And after it was sold, wasn't the money at your disposal? What made you think of doing such a thing? You have not lied to men but to God. 5 When Ananias heard this, he fell down and died. And great fear seized all who heard what had happened. 6

Then the young men came forward, wrapped up his body, and carried him out and buried him. 7 About three hours later his wife came in, not knowing what had happened. 8 Peter asked her, "Tell me, is this the price you and Ananias got for the land?"

2 Tim 4:14 Alexander the metal worker did me a great deal of harm. The Lord will repay him for what he has done.

Acts 19:30-37 Paul wanted to appear before the crowd, but the disciples would not let him. 31 Even some of the officials of the province, friends of Paul, sent him a message begging him not to venture into the theater. 32 The assembly was in confusion: Some were shouting one thing, some another. Most of the people did not even know why they were there. 33 The Jews pushed Alexander to the front, and some of the crowd shouted instructions to him. He motioned for silence in order to make a defense before the people. 34 But when they realized he was a Jew, they all shouted in unison for about two hours: "Great is Artemis of the Ephesians!" 35 The city clerk quieted the crowd and said: "Men of Ephesus, doesn't all the world know that the city of Ephesus is the guardian of the temple of the great Artemis and of her image, which fell from heaven? 36 Therefore, since these facts are undeniable, you ought to be quiet and not do anything rash. 37 You have brought these men here, though they have neither robbed temples nor blasphemed our goddess. (NIV)

He mentions Alexander, and the mischief that he had done him. This is he who is spoken of in Acts 19:33. It should seem he had been a professor of the Christian religion, for he was there particularly maligned by the worshippers of Diana, and yet he did Paul much evil. Paul foretells that God would reckon with him.

It is a prophetical denunciation of the just judgment of God that would befall him: The Lord will reward him according to his works. He cautions Timothy to take heed of him: "Of whom be thou aware also, that he does not, under presence of friendship, betray thee to mischief."

It is dangerous having anything to do with those who would be enemies to such a man as Paul.

Observe how the apostles of the early church dealt with constant adversity and conflict. Paul was in as much danger from false brethren 2 Cor. 11:26 as from open enemies, as well as from his own countrymen.

2 Corinthians 11:26-27 NIV

> I have been constantly on the move. I have been in danger from

- rivers,
- bandits,
- my own countrymen,
- Gentiles;
- the city,
- the country,
- at sea; and
- from false brothers.

(1) I have labored and toiled and I have often gone without sleep; I have known hunger and thirst, and I have often gone without food; I have been cold and naked. Some who were once Paul's hearers and admirers did not give him reason to remember them with much pleasure. For one forsook him, and another did him much evil, and greatly withstood his words.

(2) At the same time he mentions some with pleasure; not allowing the badness of some to make him forget the goodness of others; ie; Timothy, Titus, Mark, and Luke. (3.) The apostle has left a brand on the names and memory of two persons; the one is Demas, who forsook him, having loved the present world, and the

other is Alexander, who greatly withstood his words. (4.) God will reward evil-doers, particularly apostates, according to their works. (5.) Of such as are of Alexander's spirit and temper, we should beware; for they will do us no good, but all the mischief that is in their power.

Acts 13:6-12 NIV

6 They traveled through the whole island until they came to Paphos. There they met a Jewish sorcerer and false prophet named Bar-Jesus, 7 who was an attendant of the proconsul, Sergius Paulus? The proconsul, an intelligent man, sent for Barnabas and Saul because he wanted to hear the word of God. 8 But Elymas the sorcerer (for that is what his name means) opposed them and tried to turn the proconsul from the faith. 9 Then Saul, who was also called Paul, filled with the Holy Spirit, looked straight at Elymas and said, 10 You are a child of the devil and an enemy of everything that is right! You are full of all kinds of deceit and trickery. Will you never stop perverting the right ways of the Lord? 11 Now the hand of the Lord is against you. You are going to be blind, and for a time you will be unable to see the light of the sun." Immediately mist and darkness came over him, and he groped about, seeking someone to lead him by the hand. 12 When the proconsul saw what had happened, he believed, for he was amazed at the teaching about the Lord. (NIV)

Elymas the Sorcerer

PAPHOS [PAY fuhs] (meaning unknown) a city on the southwestern extremity of the island of Cyprus (see Map 7, D-2). Paul, Barnabas, and John visited Paphos during Paul's first missionary journey, about A. D. 47 or 48, Acts 13:6-13. Two settlements in the same general area of Cyprus are known as Old Paphos (modern Konklia), and New Paphos, about 16 kilometers (10 miles) to the northwest. New Paphos is the Paphos mentioned in the Book of Acts (modern Baffa).

At Paphos, Paul met the Roman proconsul Sergius Paulus, who believed the gospel Acts 13:12 when he witnessed Paul's rebuke of Elymas the sorcerer.

3 John 1: 9-11 (KJV) I wrote unto the church: but Diotrephes, who loveth to have the preeminence among them, receiveth us not. (an ugly, bad spirited person, who, as sometimes happens, ends up in leadership and causes division) 10 Wherefore, if I come, I will remember his deeds which he doeth, Prating against us with malicious words: and not content therewith, neither doth he himself receive the brethren, and forbiddeth them that would, and casteth them out of the church. 11 Beloved, follow not that which is evil, (apparently we all can be fooled) but that which is good. He that doeth good is of God: but he that doeth evil hath not seen God. (even if they are in leadership within the church)

Diotrophes is indicative of a bad attitude that often accompanies a hidden agenda that may serve his personal agenda made up of carnal desires. The problem is that this attitude may even prevail in leadership today. This carnal spirit may even be present in those professing to represent the gospel in ministry, (preaching, teaching & in leading praise and worship). While giving the appearance of defending the church, in reality it is possible that it is his/her own spirit and agenda, that he or she may be promoting.

1 Tim 1: 18-20 (KJV) This charge I commit unto thee, son Timothy, according to the prophecies which went before on thee, that thou by them mightest war a good warfare; 19 Holding faith, and a good conscience; which some having put away concerning faith have made shipwreck: 20 Of whom is Hymenaeus and Alexander; whom I have delivered unto Satan, that they may learn not to blaspheme.

2 Tim 2:16-19 (KJV) But shun profane and vain babblings: for they will increase unto more ungodliness. 17 And their word will eat as doth a canker: of whom is Hymenaeus and Philetus; 18 Who concerning the truth have erred, saying that the resurrection is past already; and overthrow the faith

of some. 19 Nevertheless the foundation of God standeth sure, having this seal, The Lord knoweth them that are his. And, Let everyone that names the name of Christ depart from iniquity.

Simon the Sorcerer

Acts 8: 9 Now for some time a man named Simon had practiced sorcery in the city and amazed all the people of Samaria. He boasted that he was someone great, 10 and all the people, both high and low, gave him their attention and exclaimed, "This man is the divine power known as the Great Power." 11 They followed him because he had amazed them for a long time with his magic. 12 But when they believed Philip as he preached the good news of the kingdom of God and the name of Jesus Christ, they were baptized, both men and women. 13 Simon himself believed and was baptized. And he followed Philip everywhere, astonished by the great signs and miracles he saw. 14 When the apostles in Jerusalem heard that Samaria had accepted the word of God, they sent Peter and John to them. 15 When they arrived, they prayed for them that they might receive the Holy Spirit, 16 because the Holy Spirit had not yet come upon any of them; they had simply been baptized into the name of the Lord Jesus. 17 Then Peter and John placed their hands on them, and they received the Holy Spirit. 18 When Simon saw that the Spirit was given at the laying on of the apostles' hands, he offered them money 19 and said, "Give me also this ability so that everyone on whom I lay my hands may receive the Holy Spirit." 20 Peter answered: "May your money perish with you, because you thought you could buy the gift of God with money! 21 You have no part or share in this ministry, because your heart is not right before God. 22 Repent of this wickedness and pray to the Lord. Perhaps he will forgive you for having such a thought in your heart. 23 For I see that you are full of bitterness and captive to sin. 24 Then Simon answered, "Pray to the Lord for me so that nothing you have said may happen to me." 25

When they had testified and proclaimed the word of the Lord, Peter and John returned to Jerusalem, preaching the gospel in many Samaritan villages.

Acts 16:16-25 Once when we were going to the place of prayer, we were met by a slave girl who had a spirit by which she predicted the future. She earned a great deal of money for her owners by fortune-telling. 17 This girl followed Paul and the rest of us, shouting, "These men are servants of the Most High God, who are telling you the way to be saved." 18 She kept this up for many days. Finally Paul became so troubled that he turned around and said to the spirit, "In the name of Jesus Christ I command you to come out of her!" At that moment the spirit left her. 19 When the owners of the slave girl realized that their hope of making money was gone, they seized Paul and Silas and dragged them into the marketplace to face the authorities. 20 They brought them before the magistrates and said, "These men are Jews, and are throwing our city into an uproar 21 by advocating customs which are unlawful for us to accept or practice." 22 The crowd joined in the attack against Paul and Silas, and the magistrates ordered them to be stripped and beaten. 23 After they had been severely flogged, they were thrown into prison, and the jailer was commanded to guard them carefully. 24 Upon receiving such orders, he put them in the inner cell and fastened their feet in the stocks. 25 About midnight Paul and Silas were praying and singing hymns to God, and the other prisoners were listening to them.

Demos

(Departed to Thessalonica, having loved this
present world more than the things of God)

It must have been a severe disappointment to the Apostle Paul when Demos departed. Especially when he left even after all that had been done for him. There is no doubt that when experiencing the same loss many times over years of pastoring, it is so easy to blame yourself when someone leaves, and I often did. However, there are times when nothing you can do or say will satisfy someone who has allowed their thoughts and actions to be caught up in a desire for the immediate satisfaction of this world. This is especially true during weak or vulnerable times and seems to bring a temptation that some cannot overcome.

It certainly points out vividly the need for His anointing on our lives. I would like to point out here that Jesus in the Gospel of John expressed his own thoughts about his personal spiritual strength. He states, "I can of mine own self do nothing". If Jesus, emptying Himself of His Godly prerogatives as we read in Philippians, known as the Kenosis, or as the self-emptying of Christ, needed the anointing of the Holy Spirit for His ministry, how much more do we that are in any form of leadership, need that same anointing.

Since I looked for a satisfying definition of the word anointing that I never could find, I decided to ask the Holy Spirit to help me identify what that experience involved. It was at that time that the following revelation came to my heart, I believe, right from the heart of God. These were the words that I understood were spoken to my heart.

"Son, the anointing is that special enduement of power from on high that helps us to accomplish in and through His Holy Spirit, what we could not accomplish in our own flesh".

In my humble opinion, we, in our own strength, are no match for the devil, but I agree with the Apostle Paul, as stated in the book of Philippians, 4:13 "I can do all things through Christ who strengthens me".

Judas Iscariot

A betrayer of the innocent blood

Matt 26:14-16 NIV Then one of the Twelve, the one called JUDAS Iscariot, went to the chief priests 15 and asked, "What are you willing to give me if I hand him over to you?" So they counted out for him thirty silver coins. 16 From then on JUDAS watched for an opportunity to hand him over.

Matt 26:18-30 NIV He replied, "Go into the city to a certain man and tell him, 'The Teacher says: My appointed time is near. I am going to celebrate the Passover with my disciples at your house.'" 19 So the disciples did as Jesus had directed them and prepared the Passover. 20 When evening came, Jesus was reclining at the table with the Twelve. 21 And while they were eating, he said, "I tell you the truth, one of you will betray me." 22 They were very sad and began to say to him one after the other, "Surely not I, Lord?" 23 Jesus replied, "The one who has dipped his hand into the bowl with me will betray me. 24 The Son of Man will go just as it is written about him. But woe to that man who betrays the Son of Man! It would be better for him if he had not been born." 25 Then JUDAS, the one who would betray him, said, "Surely not I, Rabbi?" Jesus answered, "Yes, it is you." 26 While they were eating, Jesus took bread, gave thanks and broke it, and gave it to his disciples, saying, "Take and eat; this is my body." 27 Then he took the cup, gave thanks and offered it to them, saying, "Drink from it, all of you. 28 This is my blood of the covenant, which is poured out for many for the forgiveness of sins. 29 I tell you, I will not drink of this fruit of the vine from now on until that day when I drink it anew with you in my Father's kingdom." 30 When they had sung a hymn, they went out to the Mount of Olives.

Matt 26:45-50 Then he returned to the disciples and said to them, "Are you still sleeping and resting? Look, the hour is near, and the Son of Man is betrayed into the hands of sinners. 46 Rise, let us go! Here comes my betrayer!" 47 While he was still speaking, JUDAS, one of the Twelve, arrived. With him was a large crowd armed with swords and clubs, sent from the chief priests and the elders of the people. 48 Now the betrayer had arranged a signal with them: "The one I kiss is the man; arrest him." 49 Going at once to Jesus, JUDAS said, "Greetings, Rabbi!" and kissed him. 50 Jesus replied, "Friend, do what you came for."

Then the men stepped forward, seized Jesus and arrested him. NIV

Matt 27:1-10 NIV Early in the morning, all the chief priests and the elders of the people came to the decision to put Jesus to death. 2 They bound him, led him away and handed him over to Pilate, the governor. 3 When Judas, who had betrayed him, saw that Jesus was condemned, he was seized with remorse and returned the thirty silver coins to the chief priests and the elders. 4 "I have sinned," he said, "for I have betrayed innocent blood." "What is that to us?" they replied. "That's your responsibility." 5 So Judas threw the money into the temple and left. Then he went away and hanged himself. 6 The chief priests picked up the coins and said, "It is against the law to put this into the treasury, since it is blood money." 7 So they decided to use the money to buy the potter's field as a burial place for foreigners. 8 That is why it has been called the Field of Blood to this day. 9 Then what was spoken by Jeremiah the prophet was fulfilled: "They took the thirty silver coins, the   price set on him by the people of Israel, 10 and they used them to buy the potter's field, as the Lord commanded me."

Cornelius

Acts 10:1-9 At Caesarea there was a man named Cornelius, a centurion in what was known as the Italian Regiment. 2 He and all his family were devout and God-fearing; he gave generously to those in need and prayed to God regularly. 3 One day at about three in the afternoon he had a vision. He distinctly saw an angel of God, who came to him and said, "Cornelius!" 4 Cornelius stared at him in fear. "What is it, Lord?" he asked. The angel answered, "Your prayers and gifts to the poor have come up as a memorial offering before God. 5 Now send men to Joppa to bring back a man named Simon who is called Peter. 6 He is staying with Simon the tanner, whose house is by the sea." 7 When the angel who spoke to him had gone, Cornelius called two of his servants and a devout soldier who was one of his attendants. 8 He told them everything that had happened and sent them to Joppa. 9 About noon the following day as they were on their journey and approaching the city, Peter went up on the roof to pray. (NIV)

QUESTION: How can we help? Especially those of us who are involved in church leadership, how can we protect the new convert? There are those who are wondering, "is there not a way to prepare them for the attacks that will no doubt be coming"?

Perhaps, some who may find themselves "attending houses of disagreements, instead of houses of worship. The new convert may lack the spiritual maturity that they may need to potentially make them spiritually able to defend themselves against these unexpected attacks of the enemy.

As a result, mistakes are made and unfortunately, more often than not, they are serious mistakes. Often to the point of some, especially if they were facing multiple problems, and had been looking to those that they had believed were committed by those in leadership. Those seemed, as least to some, to have become "humanly carnal". No matter who we are, or how long we have been a Christian, if we lack the anointing of His Holy Spirit, we become unarmed, and are then no match for the enemy.

Yet there are still those that even while in leadership, cannot seem to understand or even grasp the power that unity brings. However, while still in leadership, by use of a hidden agenda, continue to desire unilateral power. This carnal attitude must be recognized, and when possible, exposed. This includes those that may not be spiritually mature; but still possess a covetous attitude toward authority and want to use it to allow themselves the opportunity to share their ideas regarding the direction of their church.

When a church in conflict arises, can the casualties of the wounded be mitigated? Is it possible that the untold spiritual damage of the individuals could be preempted, minimized, or even totally prevented?

Throughout the following scriptures, the apostle Paul endeavors to speak out about what he feels is causing difficulty in some of the churches; both those he established and those that he may have helped to establish.

Acts 20:29 For I know this, that after my departing shall grievous wolves enter in among you, not sparing the flock for I knew this - or, more simply, 'I know." That, after my departing, shall grievous wolves enter in among you, not sparing the flock.

Also of your own selves shall men arise, speaking perverse (or crooked') things. 'As a member of the body may be strained and by violent bending put into a distorted position, so also truths may be perverted, placed in false relations to each other, distorted by exaggeration, changed into caricatures of that which they originally represented. And this is the nature of all false doctrine, Error is only a misrepresentation of truth; every false doctrine has some truth at bottom, which is misrepresented by the fault of men.

Perhaps the one pointed to that subtle poison of Oriental Gnosticism which we know to have very early infected the Asiatic churches; the other to such Judaizing tendencies as we know to have troubled nearly all the early churches. (See the Epistles to the Ephesians, Colossians, and Timothy; also those to the seven churches of Asia, Rev 2 and 3.)

The remedy against this, and all that tends to injure and corrupt the church now follows.

Acts 20:31-32 Therefore watch, and remember, that by the space of three years I ceased not to warn every one night and day with tears.

Therefore watch. This great duty of pastors applies to every age of the Church. And remember - keep in view, as a model which ye will do well to copy, how That by the space of three years - speaking in round numbers, it being more than two years, I ceased not to warn a word, as Alford notes, used in the New Testament only by our apostle, and by him seven times besides this. And now, brethren, I commend you to God, and to the word of his grace, which is able to build you up, and to give you an inheritance among all them which are sanctified.

It is remarkable that the only other place where this precise phrase is used is in the speech of our apostle before Agrippa (Acts 26:18), confirming the impression which this whole address conveys to the reader, that it is here recorded as delivered. And if it should be said (as the Tubingen school scruple not to do) that this only proves that both speeches proceeded from one pen-not that they were the words of Paul-then another coincidence, quite as striking, will tend to fix the Pauline authorship of both addresses: in one only of our apostle's Epistles does a phrase precisely like this occur, and that is just in his epistle to these same Ephesians (Acts 1:18), "that ye may know what is ... the riches of the glory of his inheritance among the saints" (en tois hagiois). It will be observed that sanctification is here viewed as the final character and condition of the heirs of glory, considered as one saved company".

"One would have to be extremely naïve and/or gullible to even assume that all churches are going to have the spiritual "unity" and "togetherness" that Jesus taught, and as his disciples preached. It is, however, the responsibility of those that are the called to this highest of callings, to preach and teach the Word of God as it references sanctification, taught not as what some have called "legalism", but the true definition that supports the eternal truths of separation from the world, and dedication to God. This truth is directed and taught, in both the old & new testaments; "as a doctrinal position".

I have personally asked many who have used the words legalism, or legalistic, to explain exactly what they mean by using the words. This is especially true when used in connection with or reference to the doctrine of sanctification, as taught in the Bible. I have yet, at least to this point, to hear a definition or reasonable answer, possibly due to their having just quoted someone who has used the term to defend some of their own personal shortcomings, or possibly even some otherwise questionable and unscriptural actions.

2 Chronicles 30:12 (NIV) Also in Judah the hand of God was on the people to give them unity of mind to carry out

what the king and his officials had ordered, following the word of the Lord.

To avoid conflict, unity must still be the basis for establishing eternal values and growing a scriptural and spiritually focused church. Conflict could have roots in one or more of the positions listed below. A smaller church, as it might relate to those that qualify for leadership, could have less qualified leadership. As a result, there may be a greater potential for dominance. Unfortunately, if this agenda is not soon discovered, it may not be revealed due to the possibility of reprisal.

This is often part of the cause why an Evangelical Church, or any other gospel preaching church, may see church growth stunted hindering spiritual maturity. If this is not corrected it may continue to record an attendance in even lower numbers than they should.

Let's just pause here for a moment to look at what was taught by Jesus and his disciples regarding the need for unity, including the urgency of that need. While He was on the cross, we were on His mind. Jesus prayed for his followers just before his crucifixion.

John 17:23 *NIV I in them and you in me, may they be brought to complete unity to let the world know that you sent me,* (please take special note of the rest of this verse) and have loved them even as you have loved me. (Did you catch the end phrase of the last sentence? I repeat it for emphasis) and have loved them even as you have loved me. This is powerful!

Please note: this verse, along with the others that speak of unity, is emphasizing the need to preach and teach what Jesus taught and believed.

Rom 15:5-7 (NIV) May the God who gives endurance and encouragement give you a spirit of unity among yourselves as you follow Christ Jesus, 6 so that with one heart and mouth you may glorify the God and Father of our Lord Jesus Christ. 7 *ACCEPT ONE ANOTHER, THEN, JUST AS CHRIST ACCEPTED YOU*, in order to bring praise to God.

Please note: AS A CHILD OF GOD, WE SHOULD INDIVIDUALLY AND COLLECTIVELY STRIVE TO MAINTAIN A RIGHT ATTITUDE EXPRESSED BY THE FOLLOWING VERSES.

Ephesians 4:1-6 NIV 1 As a prisoner for the Lord, then, I urge you to live a life worthy of the calling you have received. 2 Be completely humble and gentle; be patient, bearing with one another in love. 3 Make every effort to keep the unity of the spirit through the bond of peace. 4 There is one body and one Spirit— just as you were called to one hope when you were called— 5 one Lord, one faith, one baptism; 6 one God and Father of all, who is over all and through all and in all.

Ephesians 4:9-13 NIV 9 (What does "he ascended" mean except that he also descended to the lower, earthly regions? 10 He who descended is the very one who ascended higher than all the heavens, in order to fill the whole universe.) 11 It was he who gave some to be apostles, some to be prophets, some to be evangelists, and some to be pastors and teachers, 12 to prepare God's people for works of service, so that the body of Christ may be built up 13 until we all reach unity in the faith and in the knowledge of the Son of God and become mature, attaining to the whole measure of the fullness of Christ. (Please see: Jude 24)

Col 3:12-17 NIV Therefore, as God's chosen people, holy and dearly loved, clothe yourselves with compassion, kindness, humility, gentleness and patience. 13 bear with each other and forgive whatever grievances you may have against one another. Forgive as the lord forgave you. (Note: unforgiveness or retaliation, are not options) 14 and over all these virtues put on love, which binds them all together in perfect unity. 15 Let the peace of Christ rule in your hearts, since as members of one body you were called to peace, and be thankful. 16 Let the word of Christ dwell in you richly as you teach and admonish one another with all wisdom, and as you sing psalms, hymns and spiritual songs with gratitude in your hearts to God. 17 and whatever you do, whether in word or deed, do it all in the name of the Lord Jesus, giving thanks to God the Father through him.

The question may be asked, why should I forgive? It is absolutely essential in order to remain in fellowship with the Lord. Forgiveness is not just an option, since we may not be as different from the wrong doer as we might like to think.

In Matthew 18:35 Jesus is teaching in response to a question regarding unforgiveness! Jesus said, "This is how my heavenly father will treat you unless you forgive your brother from your heart".

The MESSAGE translation by Peterson from Matt. 18 regarding the failure to forgive and its consequences gives great insight.

Forgiveness is the key component to the victorious/ overcomer. This is the way of the cross to becoming, more than conquerors. The only thing more difficult than forgiveness, is the alternative. Maybe some of us need to remind ourselves again, it is not about us, but it is, after all, all about what he did through and by his death on the cross, that through our faith in him and by confession of our sinful Adamic nature to him, forgives us, making us a child of God, by taking away our sin and writing our names in the lamb's book of life.

Chapter 1

How and From Where Does Conflict Arise?

There are many, many, committed churches and para-church organizations that are led by dedicated pastors, staff, and boards that are primarily made up of many dedicated men and women of integrity, unselfish behavior, and capable leadership. After 55 years of dealing with conflict, both with those in the ministry and in churches, (no denomination is excluded); I have listed the following positions that include members of the leadership of just about any religious organization. They can potentially allow themselves to be used by our mutual enemy, the devil, either unwittingly or with self-serving attitudes and purpose to become potential players or participators that are sometimes, even unsuspectingly, caught up in a conflict over "a quest for control."

Again, let me say at this juncture, that there are many pastors, both seniors and associates, along with many church leaders, that have been, and are today, true shepherds and disciples. They depend on him each and every day for their very existence and the success of their ministries. This does not hide the fact that there may be those in leadership in any denomination or fellowship that may be or could be deceived into thinking that they are the important ones. They make the mistake of claiming ownership, and by purposely reversing the scripture that exhorts us that he (Jesus) would increase in our lives, and we would decrease, would be reversed and allow him to decrease, and them to increase, making themselves indispensable.

The riches of this life should never be allowed to influence a congregation to allow those that use their wealth, regardless of their apparent lack of spirituality, to gain prominence or leadership in any form.

Remember: Reputation is what people think we are; character is what God knows we are.

It might be helpful if we take a look at the analogies that reference what there is about this world that can rob us of our focus on spiritual things.

> Matt 13:22 (KJV) He also that received seed among the thorns is he that heareth the word, and the care of this world, and the deceitfulness of riches, choke the word, and he becometh unfruitful.

> Mark 10:24-25 And the disciples were astonished at his words. But Jesus answereth again, and saith unto them, Children, how hard is it for them that trust in riches to enter into the kingdom of God! 25 It is easier for a camel to go through the eye of a needle, than for a rich man to enter into the kingdom of God.

> 1 Tim 6:17-18 (KJV) Charge them that are rich in this world, that they be not high-minded, nor trust in uncertain riches, but in the living God, who giveth us richly all things to enjoy; 18 that they do good, that they be rich in good works, ready to distribute, willing to communicate;

People in positions of leadership, in any church or para-church organization, should be responsible for a reasonable amount of accountability. However, there may be some that assume much more than just their understanding of what they thought their responsibilities were to be.

There is, more often than not, some system of training. This is to include, as early as possible in the establishment of any church (or para-organization), at least an outline serving as a job description. It would include a list of the duties and responsibilities relating to the specific area in which someone is being asked to serve. It should include information that would discourage those, who being in leadership, may yield to a self-serving attitude.

In addition, this job description should be reviewed and improved each year by those, by reference to their own job description, requires them to do so. This is generally discussed when it is time to consider the granting of a financial increase.

In my humble opinion, it is often possible that if there is no direction or outline of responsibilities and duties, or the parameters within which one should use to carry out their assignment, that it may open the door for frustration and perhaps even discouragement to those having that responsibility without accountability. This could ultimately result in a resignation. It may even explain for a lack of volunteers; not wanting to take on a ministry that isn't clearly defined. In some cases, it could ultimately end up that there is no or little benefit in maintaining the continued existence of the unfulfilled position or ministry; especially when the responsibilities and/or authority for such services are not clearly defined.

It is also extremely important that a church or para-church, (especially a 501-c-3 not for profit organization) be equipped with a good constitution and by-laws. In addition, at least a semblance of appropriate policies and procedures should help give direction to those who may be appointed, elected, or asked to serve in any area of leadership. This includes the Senior Pastor on down to every person who has been given or has been elected to a place of leadership. Regardless of how big or how small that church may be, it puts them among those that carry the burden of that church in particular, as well as the church in general.

Hopefully, the information contained in the job description that they receive is clear and covers the specifics, as well as the general duties and responsibilities of the position(s) or areas, in which they are asked to serve. They should also be provided, as soon as possible, an easy to understand handbook containing necessary references to the general, as well as the specific policies and procedures. This would include anything regarding the administrative areas of the church and the accepted policies and procedures recommended by the leadership responsible for those setting the policies for that congregation.

This information, while insignificant to some, may serve to prevent the possibility or at least reduce attempts by anyone involved in leadership that may endeavor to impose their unilateral will of control upon others. This is especially true if their attitude is not right and/or some begin practicing areas of control that are contrary to the Biblical principles and positions that are held, accepted, and taught by the trusted leadership of that specific congregation.

Consider with me, the apostle John's reference to a person of "ill repute," mentioned in the 3rd epistle of John.

Diotrephes: Who loves to be First

> 3 John 1:5-10 NIV Dear friend, you are faithful in what you are doing for the brothers, even though they are strangers to you. 6 They have told the church about your love. You will do well to send them on their way in a manner worthy of God. 7 It was for the sake of the Name that they went out, receiving no help from the pagans. 8 We ought therefore to show hospitality to such men so that we may work together for the truth. 9 I wrote to the church, but Diotrephes, who loves to be first, will have nothing to do with us. 10 So if I come, I will call attention to what he is doing, gossiping maliciously about us. Not satisfied with that, he refuses to welcome the brothers. He also stops those who want to do so and puts them out of the church.

Unfortunately, the casualties in most churches do not come from any one specific area of the church body. They can, in fact, be generated in several different areas and through the most unsuspecting people.

Some of which may really have their own agenda, but have given the impression that what they are doing, or proposing to do, is for the benefit and/or the protection of the congregation; members and constituents alike.

These attitudes, more often than not, tend to cause division and may result in spiritual injuries. In some cases these attitudes may result in casualties among the new converts, and even those who may have been a Christian for a while.

Oh how the gift of discernment, (not the gift of suspicion), is needed to see through those having personal or controlling motives.

In the areas of wanting or desiring to be in leadership, it might help if we first examine our purpose for wanting to serve. The following scriptures exhort us to be careful about; "Thinking more highly about ourselves than we ought."

Phil 2:3-5 NIV Do nothing out of selfish ambition or vain conceit, but in humility consider others better than yourselves. 4 Each of you should look not only to your own interests, but also to the interests of others. 5 Your attitude should be the same as that of Jesus Christ.

Those tempted to have a controlling spirit may include, but certainly may not be limited to, the following:

The Senior Pastor

The Senior Pastor (referred to in the KJV and other translations as elders or in some cases, lead pastors) are, at least in most churches, called to be under shepherds of His sheep. They are, in most cases, regarded as the spiritual leader or the lead pastoral elder. First, let's take a look at the Scriptures that strongly support faithful pastors, and there are many, and their need for being treated with love and respect, as is recorded in 1st Timothy 5:17-22, 24, 25, (TLB)

> 17 Pastors who do their work well should be paid well and should be highly appreciated, especially those who work hard at both preaching and teaching. 18 For the Scriptures say, "Never tie up the mouth of an ox when it is treading out the grain-let him eat as he goes along!" And in another place, "Those who work deserve their pay!" 19 Don't listen to complaints against the pastor unless there are two or three witnesses to accuse him. 20 If he has really sinned, then he should be rebuked in front of the whole church so that no one else will follow his example. 21 I solemnly command you in the presence of God and the Lord Jesus Christ and of the holy angels to do this (note: please make special note of the following) whether the pastor is a special friend of yours or not. All must be treated exactly the same.

Should there be an accusation against a pastor, before proceeding with any public charges, great care should be taken to learn all of the available facts. This is to protect the pastor's reputation, his standing in the community and the reputation of the church family itself. There must be unquestionable proof of any accusation or wrong doing before being openly charged with violations. The old term, "everyone is saying" is just not sufficient to jeopardize the life and the sacrificial ministry of a pastor, of any leader or member of the household of faith.

The following scriptures give good advice regarding the selection of a pastor. Remember, it is much easier to elect, than to have to request the resignation of a pastor.

> 1st Timothy 5:22, 24, 25, (TLB) Never be in a hurry about choosing a pastor; you may overlook his sins, and it will look as if you approve of them. Be sure that you yourself stay away from all sin. 24 Remember that some men, even pastors, lead sinful lives, and everyone knows it. In some situations you can do something about it. But in other cases only the judgment day will reveal the terrible truth. 25 In the same way, everyone knows how much good some pastors do, but sometimes their good deeds aren't known until long afterward.

This, in many cases, would include a potential pastor possessing a vision for the body of believers he has been called to pastor. He should be dedicated to the position he has been called to fill; and continually, along with his other pastoral duties, be looking for direction for that church's body of believers. Having been a pastor for several months, this leader should have some concepts, or at least an outline, to discuss with those in leadership regarding a short range, mid-range, and a long range plan for the spiritual, numerical, material and financial growth of that congregation. Be very aware of the need for fiscal responsibility to accompany each financial decision.

While the above is encouraged, care must be taken not to cast a vision for change too soon. It is important to not make too many changes at once, or make it difficult for the congregation to grasp how the changes will be made. It's usually best not to seek to impose personal agendas that you or the membership may need, or possibly want to be changed, at a later time.

Hopefully, at the end of the day and when the time is right, the vision will benefit the Kingdom of God in a practical way; enhancing areas of the pastorate emphasizing those ministries that will ultimately result in eternal value.

It must be emphasized here that evangelism, according to His word, should be the driving force, which should always be involved, as well as a part of the spiritual growth and development of any church.

In retrospect, when looking at the ultimate accomplishment of a spiritual vision, we need to make sure that the growth and development of His church is not merely the result of ministers who, by their very personality and marketing ability, can draw people to themselves by their personality, rather than to the Lord and His church. We must be constantly on our guard against compromise and self-indulgence. In our efforts to build a growing church, we must be watchful of those sheep that may need help in areas of spiritual weakness.

We need to constantly remind ourselves that we are pastors, called by God, to be under shepherds with Christ as our Shepherd leader. We are not just the President or even a CEO, with an MBA and a tremendous resume' of some prospering business, that happens to have a church name or an affiliation, as a 501c3, "not-for profit" church or para-church organization.

One pastor asked me if I could help him to understand why, in spite of his continuing efforts to preach the true gospel of repentance and salvation, his church was growing so slowly; especially since the newest pastor in town enjoyed a growing congregation from the time he arrived.

First of all, I mentioned to him the fallacy of comparing ourselves with others. We need to understand that God has made us as individuals, new creatures in Christ Jesus, with different gifts and potentials. The unique circumstances may be different for other churches, but it is the Holy Spirit that works through us all to accomplish His perfect will.

Secondly, since I wanted him to understand the law of sowing and reaping, I ask him what he was planting and what kind of seeds he was putting into the hearts of his congregation? Then I mention to him that anyone can grow "weeds," in fact, you don't even have to plant them; they basically come up all by themselves. The problem with weeds is evident to us all. They are really not fit for anything but to remove and burn.

I further explained that if you plant an oak tree, it would take years to grow into something that will ultimately be of use. Even as it grows, you will then see the spiritual strength, beauty, and maturity of what you have planted years later, after being nourished by the Holy Spirit.

Remember, a year old tree, especially an oak tree, can be just as healthy as one 50 years old. A healthy church is usually a growing church, but in the case of an oak, it will no doubt take a lifetime of growth and development to reach complete maturity.

> The Apostle Paul declares in his epistle to the church at Philippi, 3:12-14 TLB I don't mean to say I am perfect. I haven't learned all I should even yet, but I keep working toward that day when I will finally be all that Christ saved me for and wants me to be. 13 No, dear brothers, I am still not all I should be, but I am bringing all my energies to bear on this one thing: Forgetting the past and looking forward to what lies ahead, I strain to reach the end of the race and receive the prize for which God is calling us up to heaven because of what Christ Jesus did for us.

Remember the adage which is still true today;

> "Only one life twill soon be past,
> Only what's done for Christ will last."

Chapter 2

The Need for A Spiritual Hospital

The church should not be a rest home for the well and strong, but a hospital that cares for those who know that they are spiritually ill. During the last 38 years of traveling, when anyone asked me what I was doing, I would, in a jesting and kidding way say, "I endeavor to diagnose "staph" infection in churches, meaning "staff" of course. As you probably noticed, it is spelled differently than the hospital term.

I had no idea how beautifully Mr. Peterson, the editor of "the message," had put into words what I was trying to express regarding what our ministry was really all about. The following is from an introduction to the book of Jude, from Peterson's *The Message*. He titled it "Diagnosing Church Diseases."

"Our spiritual communities are as susceptible to disease as our physical bodies. But it is easier to detect whatever is wrong in our stomachs and lungs than in our worship and witness. When our physical bodies are sick or damaged, the pain calls our attention to it, and we do something as quickly as possible. But a dangerous, and even a more deadly virus in our spiritual communities, can go undetected for a long time. As much as we need physicians for our bodies, we have an even greater need for diagnosticians and healers of the spirit.

Jude's letter to an early community of Christians is just such a diagnosis. It is all the more necessary in that those believers apparently didn't know anything was even wrong, or at least not as desperately wrong as Jude points out. There is, of course, far more to living in a Christian community than protecting the faith against assault or subversion. Paranoia is as unhealthy spiritually as it is mentally. The primary Christian posture is, in Jude's words, "keeping your arms open and outstretched, ready for the mercy of our master Jesus Christ. All the same, energetic watchfulness is required.   Jude's whistle-blowing has prevented many a disaster".

May we all take heed to the admonition of Paul to the Corinthian Church.

"I appeal to you, dear brothers and sisters, by the authority of our Lord Jesus Christ, to live in harmony with each other. Let there be no divisions in the church. Rather, be of one mind, united in thought and purpose. For some members of Chloe's household have told me about your quarrels, my dear brothers and sisters. Some of you are saying, "I am a follower of Paul." Others are saying, "I follow Apollos," or "I follow Peter," or "I follow only Christ."

Has Christ been divided into factions? Was I, Paul, crucified for you? Were any of you baptized in the name of Paul? Of course not! I thank God that I did not baptize any of you except Crispus and Gaius, for now no one can say they were baptized in my name. (Oh yes, I also baptized the household of Stephanas, but I don't remember baptizing anyone else.) For Christ didn't send me to baptize, but to preach the Good News—and not with clever speech, for fear that the cross of Christ would lose its power.

The message of the cross is foolish to those who are headed for destruction! But we who are being saved know it is the very power of God. As the Scriptures say,

"I will destroy the wisdom of the wise and discard the intelligence of the intelligent."

So where does this leave the philosophers, the scholars, and the world's brilliant debaters? God has made the wisdom of this world look foolish. Since God in his wisdom saw to it that the world would never know him through human wisdom, he has used our foolish preaching to save those who believe. It is foolish to the Jews, who ask for signs from heaven. And it is foolish to the Greeks, who seek human wisdom. So when we preach that Christ was crucified, the Jews are offended and the Gentiles say it's all nonsense.

But to those called by God to salvation, both Jews and Gentiles, Christ is the power of God and the wisdom of God. This foolish plan of God is wiser than the wisest of human plans, and God's weakness is stronger than the greatest of human strength.

Remember, dear brothers and sisters, that few of you were wise in the world's eyes or powerful or wealthy when God called you. Instead, God chose things the world considers foolish in order to shame those who think they are wise. And he chose things that are powerless to shame those who are powerful. God chose things despised by the world; things counted as nothing at all, and used them to bring to nothing what the world considers important. As a result, no one can ever boast in the presence of God.

God has united you with Christ Jesus. For our benefit God made him to be wisdom itself. Christ made us right with God; he made us pure and holy, and he freed us from sin. Therefore, as the Scriptures say, "If you want to boast, boast only about the Lord." 1 Cor. 1:10-30

Conflict in the life of the church is nothing new. However, conflict must be resolved in a biblical way in order for the church to fulfill its purpose in our generation.

Unity is Essential

If we are members of his body, how then can we continue to separate the parts according to our particular personal agenda? If we use the word "body" in connection with the ownership of "his church", I feel sure that it would be kind of hard for anyone of us to say it was ours. Every labor in the vineyard of God has a place, a purpose and calling. We are members one of another, and are to work together for the glory of God.

1 Cor 3:6-9 (KJV)

6 I have planted, Apollos watered; but God gave the increase. 7 So then neither is he that planteth anything, neither he that watereth; BUT GOD that giveth the increase.

8 Now he that planteth and he that watereth are one: and every man shall receive his own reward according to his own labour. 9 For we are labourers together with God: ye are God's husbandry, ye are God's building.

To say that unity is essential means that disunity is destructive. It is a sad commentary, but nonetheless true, that Sunday morning is the most segregated time of the week in the American church. The concept of a White church, Black church, Asian church...there is only one church expressed via local churches in communities everywhere. Unity does not mean we have to do everything the same, for unity in diversity is a beautiful picture of all God has created. Conflict is probably inevitable in the church, but our goal should be to resolve conflict as soon as possible so the vision of the Kingdom is never divided or disturbed.

Chapter 3

The Wisdom of James

Presented here is an introduction to the book of James from Peterson's *The Message* titled "Diagnosing Church Infections."

"The letter of James shows one of the church's early pastors skillfully going about his work of confronting, diagnosing, and dealing with areas of misbelief and misbehavior that had turned up in congregations committed to his care. When Christian believers gather in churches, everything that can go wrong, sooner or later does. Outsiders on observing this, conclude that there is nothing to the religion business except perhaps business-and dishonest business at that. Insiders see it differently. Just as the hospital collects its sick under one roof and labels them as such, the church collects sinners. Many of the people outside of the hospital are every bit as sick as the ones inside, but their illnesses are either undiagnosed or disguised. It's similar with sinners outside the church. So Christian churches are not, as a rule, model communities of good behavior. They are places where human misbehavior is brought out in the open, faced, and dealt with.

The letter of James shows one of the church's early pastors skillfully going about his work of confronting, diagnosing, and dealing with areas of misbelief and misbehavior that had turned up in congregations committed to his care.

Deep and living wisdom is on display here. Wisdom is both rare and essential. However wisdom is not primarily knowing the truth, although it certainly includes that. It is skill in living. What good is a truth if we don't know how to live it? What good is an intention if we can't sustain it?

Those serving in a pastoral position of any stature are expected to be men or woman of integrity, doing their best to fulfill the commands of Jesus, especially the one regarding our natural affections.

We can do no greater while on this earth than to keep our focus on Heaven and all that it has to offer. The choice of heaven or hell should still be made in light of what Jesus has promised and will perform."

Col 3:1-3 (NIV)

1 Since, then, you have been raised with Christ, set your hearts on things above, where Christ is seated at the right hand of God. 2 Set your minds on things above, not on earthly things. 3 For you died, and your life is now hidden with Christ in God.

Matt 6:19-21

19 Lay not up for yourselves treasures upon earth, where moth and rust doth corrupt, and where thieves break through and steal: 20 But lay up for yourselves treasures in heaven, where neither moth nor rust doth corrupt, and where thieves do not break through nor steal: 21 FOR WHERE YOUR TREASURE IS, THERE WILL YOUR HEART BE ALSO. (Authors emphasis)

Ultimately, disunity and conflict are a heart issue. It has been said that if someone can be offended, they will be offended. Wounds and offenses do occur in church, but if our hearts are right before the Lord, and we focus on loving each other not fixing each other, wounds can be avoided and offenses dealt with in a healthy and positive fashion.

Chapter 4

The Value of Experience

In some cases, experience is still the best teacher!

There are many pastors, at all levels of leadership, who started out in the ministry wholly dedicated to his plan and purpose, enthused by the thought of working in unity with other Christians. However, it doesn't take long to realize that just because we are in any form of leadership, or have REV. in front of our name, that we, in any ministry, even among professed Christians, will always be working side by side with even "near perfect" or "completely mature," men and women.

My first several months of Bible College became a revelation to me. I had just been saved a year or two and while I had my struggles, I had a strong desire to have Him, through His Holy Spirit, guide my life and bring conviction to any part of my life that needed to be changed. I had no idea at the time, how much it needed to be changed.

One of my most embarrassing experiences came during that first year of my attendance to a Bible College. This experience was to serve me well and affect me for the rest of my life. It certainly taught me a lesson that I remember to this day.

As difficult as it is, even now, to share these times of learning, I want to make this known, because it's possible that some of you reading this now may be experiencing similar situations. Hopefully, at whatever spiritual place we are, we may all have benefited from our mistakes.

After spending time with other students, I began to notice expressions and words among the things that I had been delivered from, being said and done. I had no idea I would see or hear these expressed at a Bible College. My strong sense of right and wrong continued to build up in me, and I became greatly disturbed over the whole issue of right living.

In my distress, watching and listening to the actions of others, I finally decided to approach the academic dean. I asked him if he knew what was going on in a professed Christian College that I thought was spiritually and physically committed to preparing students for the ministry.

He asked me why I was asking such a question. I proceeded to unburden by heart about the "actions and conversations" of others. I explained that I didn't expect to find these things in a Bible College setting.

He listen intently to my description of what I felt was "over the top" for those that were involved. I tried to make it clear that I didn't come to him with a critical spirit, but because I was disappointed and concerned about what I was seeing and hearing.

After he had listened to my "tales of woe," he responded. It was an answer that I had not expected and was really not prepared to hear.

He said, "Well my brother, if you expected this to be a college of perfect people, you should have known better when God called you." That really ended the conversation. Not knowing what else to say, I left his office, not only embarrassed, but feeling that I had just been hit by a truck.

I am not sure he really understood the effect his words had on me. One thing is for sure, it straightened me out regarding what I was to expect during the rest of my college years and in the ministry during the years to come. Never again did I go to him or anyone else with these problems that had grown out of what I had heard preached and then adopted as my own personal standards of righteousness and/or views of holiness.

I needed to deal with my own focus and what the scriptures enjoined me to do. This made me aware of my own life and responsibilities for personal obedience to His call. The words of Isaiah 6 had a lasting effect on me. This verse helped me keep my mind straight and upon His plan for me, as I endeavored to follow him.

ISA 6:5-8 (KJV)

5 Then said I, Woe is me! for I am undone; because I am a man of unclean lips, and I dwell in the midst of a people of unclean lips: for mine eyes have seen the King, the LORD of hosts. 6 Then flew one of the seraphims unto me, having a live coal in his hand, which he had taken with the tongs from off the altar: 7 And he laid it upon my mouth, and said, Lo, this hath touched thy lips; and thine iniquity is taken away, and thy sin purged. 8 Also I heard the voice of the Lord, saying, "Whom shall I send, and who will go for us?" Then said I, Here am I; send me.

While the past has not been easy for anyone, we must learn with the Apostle Paul as recorded in his letter to the church at Philippi, forgetting those things that are behind, and pressing on to prize of the high calling of Christ Jesus. Serving the Lord as Savior, and allow that scripture to settle it for me. "Here am I Lord, send me". Allowing other Scriptures, like the following ones, to have their effect on me as well.

Jer 29:11-13 (TLB)

11 "For I know the plans I have for you," says the Lord. "They are plans for good and not for evil, to give you a future and a hope. 12 In those days when you pray, I will listen. 13 You will find me when you seek me, if you look for me in earnest."

An under shepherd should be excited about preaching. He or she needs to focus on prayer, the study of His Word, and most of all have a continued vision and dream with an unceasing eternal hope for the salvation of lost souls. Making sure that he keeps his focus on Him and the eternal values He has set before us.

After serving for many years in the pastoral ministry and during my tenure on a leadership board in 1958, I was asked by the District Superintendent if I would accept a committee chairman appointment. I was to appoint my own committee members and submit a "white paper" describing what we concluded were the most difficult aspects of the ministry.

I took that challenge, and our committee described in writing, as best we could, the following, areas that we felt contributed to the demise of some pastors, churches and/or even denominations.

Having been involved with district appointments since 1980 as an interim pastor, it was my responsibility to try and diagnose what the real problems were, and then help provide a solution. We felt that many of the more difficult problems were often found in the smaller churches. This was not to say that some of the larger churches did not fall victim to challenging times as a result of individual or group conflicts.

Unfortunately, in all too many churches, what we had written became even more of a reality than I expected. The following is the essence of what we felt was the most difficult areas. Not to say that there were no other serious conflicts. We continued to describe in writing what we felt to be some of the more difficult problems as briefly referred to by the following.

 In all too many churches, familiarity has bred contempt because of doing the same things year after year without consulting the Holy Spirit about what may need to be changed.

Spiritual fatigue or becoming spiritually worn out, is a real problem for many a servant of the Lord. There are those who get involved in so many different ministries that they don't even have time to attend services. Then some claim ownership of a particular ministry and end up becoming involved in areas of constant conflict. When there is conflict, circumstances often lead to the resignation of people in all areas of ministry. This is generally followed by a spirit of apathy within the body. Apathy from among the congregation becomes a tool of the enemy. It leads to not only affecting those in the congregation, but also infecting those in leadership. This may be accompanied by becoming burned out. Thus it causes a loss of vision to those in leadership that are involved in both church and para-church organizations.

It is About Jesus

Those who claim ownership of any church will one day be very disappointed with that claim. A battle of human wills may exist in some churches, especially in the area of those desiring administrative positions; or in those who would later, under the pretences of "protecting the church." They may by plan, or even unintentionally begin to display a controlling spirit.

Over time, should this continue, it will become increasing more evident. The "CONFLICT" will begin to surface due to a spirit of control." This will often begin with a person in leadership, or a small group, whom the pastor may have put his confidence in too quickly. It doesn't take long for this kind of spirit to show its deceitful head. It may be exacerbated by those who do not really care about the future impact of what is happening. This may include the possibility of mortally wounding a few people or many, especially the new converts.

Behind closed doors, this can cause some who have attended for years to threaten either a split, or in an effort to get their own way, the destruction or injury in part or in all of the entire congregation. It could take years to recover, if ever.

While speaking at ministers meetings in different parts of the country, I have endeavored to encourage the pastors to offer communion during both board meetings and business meetings. The Holy Spirit should be invited to attend, and we should welcome His presence in whatever services we have. He is our Lord.

Chapter 5

Pride Comes...then the Fall

At times, a problem with arrogance may exist among the saints. In the first letter to the church at Corinth, the apostle Paul points out to the entire church that they have a real problem with arrogance.

1 Cor. 4:14-21

> 14 I am not writing this to shame you, but to warn you, as my dear children. 15 Even though you have ten thousand guardians in Christ, you do not have many fathers, for in Christ Jesus I became your father through the gospel. 16 Therefore I urge you to imitate me. 17 For this reason I am sending to you Timothy, my son whom I love, who is faithful in the Lord. He will remind you of my way of life in Christ Jesus, which agrees with what I teach everywhere in every church. 18 Some of you have become arrogant, as if I were not coming to you. 19 But I will come to you very soon, if the Lord is willing, and then I will find out not only how these arrogant people are talking, but what power they have. 20 For the kingdom of God is not a matter of talk but of power. 21 What do you prefer? Shall I come to you with a whip, or in love and with a gentle spirit?

If the new pastor is young and inexperienced, armed only with a Bible and a sincere burden for souls, he/she or their spouse may be unable to make any changes without consulting those who have been in control for years. This may be true even if they are legitimate needs. Those who have already been in control may not be willing to give up their position of authority, even if it would be an improvement over what they consider to be their particular area of "ministry."

The apostles lead by example, not by a spirit of control. (1 Cor. 3:9 TLB) The Apostle Paul took ownership of nothing. It all belonged to his Lord. We are only God's coworkers. You are God's garden, not ours; you are God's building, NOT OURS.

This spirit of control and/or a desire for authority is not limited to just the members of the congregation in general, but even more importantly, may exist in the leadership, and in some cases, I am sorry to say it may include a pastor or members of the pastoral staff.

In the Word of God, there is a direct reference to such a battle for control. May the Lord help us to learn from the mistakes of the early church leaders as well as our own more contemporary shortcomings.

In the following pages, we will make an attempt to draw our attention to the diseases that seem to be endemic to evangelical, as well as many other historic church bodies. In my humble opinion, having ministered in these areas, I now recognize that presently this spiritual disease is growing in an alarming percentage of church bodies, as well as the para-church organizations.

Chapter 6

More Experience

In one of our first pastorates, my attitude needed help; I was to stand for election each year. This was due to a previous pastor who refused to leave after some 13 years, in spite of the fact that the congregation was dwindling and he was believed to be legally blind.

The otherwise dedicated men, who came from that church to establish another church, now seemed highly defensive due to their previous experience; especially in response to any pastor who may want to be elected for an indefinite period.

After some 3 ½ years, and in spite of our having a growing and blessed church, I became somewhat frustrated over this position. Not that I had anything in my heart toward their decisions, but it was more about my having to pay the price for not having the trust that had been lost under another totally different set of circumstances.

During the following explanation of what had taken place in the past three years, (please notice the amount of times "I" have included the "big I") I attempted to change what "I" thought to be unfair.

At the upcoming business meeting, I had made up my mind that I was going to ask for an indefinite period. (Incidentally, since then I have had communion served at the beginning of some business and board meetings. You may be surprised at how attitudes change when His presence is practiced in these meetings other than those held for the regular church services.) I discussed this with the board. During those 3 years, the church had grown substantially and I had set my mind to have that rule changed. Feeling that they were penalizing me for what had happened to them in the past, I felt it only fair to have their previous decision changed.

It is important to note here that there were several Board Members who were vehemently opposed. They expressed their feelings regarding such a decision. One board member asked me, "What is going to happen if you don't get the indefinite vote, will you still stay?" Feeling that my decision to ask for the indefinite vote was right, I told him as humbly as I could. "I will decide that at the meeting, depending on the vote count."

I am sure that some of the board members left feeling that I had violated what they felt was right, and they would stand against it in the business meeting. But my mind was made up, this was going to happen. I had waited 3 years. Their present positon was wrong and needed to be changed now.

I used the legitimate excuse that I needed to do this in my own defense. So due to my trepidation about my position, my logic told me that if there came a time when some serious violations occurred involving some of the members, and that known practiced sin was indeed in need of discipline, there could be a problem.

If I proceeded to take the steps necessary to correct such practiced sin, those being disciplined may allow their feeling to dictate how they would vote, and be sharing this with others. This could negatively affect the vote. In all honesty, looking back in retrospect, I'm afraid I didn't seek the Lord more earnestly for His plan. Thank God HE is the discerner of not only our thoughts, but the intent of our heart.

However, there was also another frustration. When I would hug or kiss one of the babies, there were those who would say in a humorous way, "Oh, it must be election time again." Boy did that have an adverse effect on me. But by then, things were about to change. I had convinced myself that I was forced to make a choice, one that would directly affect my own personal and spiritual maturity.

I believe it was about to be made clear to me. His Holy Spirit began to speak to me in a way I had never known. It all started the night before the business meeting was to be held. As far as I knew, I was facing it with an open heart. I had made up my mind that I was not going to let a few people in authority decide what I felt most of the congregation would want changed.

However, that night I had a most powerful dream. This dream was to change my entire outlook on that business meeting and all the Board and Business meetings that followed. I am so glad that while man may look on the outward appearance, the Lord looks on the heart. He knew that I wanted to be a true shepherd, not a hireling, and that I wanted His will for me personally regardless of the cost.

Well, in this dream, which seemed almost as though it was real, I experienced something that I have not had repeated in that manner from then till now. I don't remember where my dream even took place; I only remember the message that was sent to me through it.

I dreamt that I was in a meeting, and that it took place in a room somewhere. I believe it was after something that I or someone else had said, that someone broke open a glass bottle and grabbed my left arm. Using the razor sharp edge of the broken glass bottle, he then proceeded to cut my arm from my elbow to my wrist. I have no recollection of who it was.

I know it might sound gross, but in my dream I could see the inside of my arm and the blood flowing from it." I woke up still holding my left arm and realizing that if that had really happened; my physical strength would be taken away. When I awakened, I was somewhat shook up, and sat on the edge of my bed. When I regained my proper senses, I asked out loud, "Lord, what just happened to me"? I don't believe I will ever forget (what I perceived to be) the word of the Lord that came to my heart that morning. What I heard in my heart of hearts was the following:

> "Son, so shall it happen to you, if you continue to want your own way and not depend on me. You will lose the strength I have given you to serve my people. It was your left arm, not your right, so you will still have strength left in your right arm, but if you continue to "want your own way, whether it be right or not, great damage will be done to my body the church, and to the ministry I have blessed you with."

That night as the business meeting began, the people had enjoyed services that were never plagued with controversy. We had had sweet peace and people were being converted and growing. Now something was apparently about to change. I could sense the concern and the tension that was on the minds of the people, as well as seen on some of their faces. I had not yet discovered the blessing of His peace that is present in a communion service, even during a business meeting.

We started with a time of praise and worship, had the reading of the previous minutes, and passed out an agenda outlining what was to happen during the meeting and what was to be involved. Thank the Lord, I had already prayed through and had accepted what I felt was a word of direct revelation and intervention from the Lord.

As the meeting progressed to the actual new business part, I announced to the members present that I had something very important I needed to say before we actually proceeded with the rest of the meeting. It became so silent that you could have just about heard a pin drop.

I began by saying, "I had been talking to our Heavenly Father, and I have received instructions that I am not to proceed with the vote that may allow me to be elected for an indefinite period, but I am to leave this in His hands for His resolution at a later time." After hearing a very distinct sigh of relief from some, and a smile from others, the business meeting continued without incident.

Now for the end of the story.

One year later, the question was raised again by members of the congregation, and my wife and I received an almost unanimous vote of confidence for an indefinite tenure. The following year, feeling it was the will of God, we resigned and became evangelists. A while later I was asked to take a church in California, where we remained for 13 ½ years, which is another incredible story in itself.

Just an aside: After being at that church in Chula Vista, CA. for several months, I was attending a banquet for the District Superintendent who had appointed me to that church.

While I was having dinner, I was approached by another preacher who knelt down beside my chair to have a word with me, and whispered in my ear these words.

"How did a preacher from Virginia get appointed to a church in Southern California?" He went on to say, "I live in Arizona and have tried for years to get a church in S. Cal. District with no success."

While not wanting to appear unkind, I asked him to bend his ear down so I could whisper the answer to him. The answer was, "I never tried".

End of story

Chapter 7

What is Synergism and How to Make It Work in a Spiritual Setting

All through the Bible we see evidence that it took more than just one man to establish leadership as recorded in both the Old and New Testaments. In many cases, there were many who worked together to accomplish God's purpose for HIS people. While there may have been one dedicated person in charge, he or she generally worked through a plurality of talents and ministries.

Psalm 133 (A song of David)

How good and pleasant it is when brothers live together in unity! It is like precious oil poured on the head, running down on the beard, running down on Aaron's beard, down upon the collar of his robes. It is as if the dew of Hermon were falling on Mount Zion. For there the LORD bestows his blessing, even life forevermore. (NIV)

Since we are the body of Christ, would it be a stretch to say that we can expect that anointing to flow down over His church as well?

May I take a moment here to address the meaning of anointing? I had looked for a number of years for a definition of anointing. I must have looked in the wrong places, because I could not find one that I felt was in keeping with my sense of what anointing should be. Finally, I decided to give it a try myself and came up with this explanation. Remember what Jesus said about his own strength, "I can of mine own self do nothing". He too needed power from on high to carry out His father's will. It was after His baptism by John that Jesus was filled with the Spirit and began His ministry. He proclaimed later that "The Spirit of the Lord is upon me for He had anointed me to preach the gospel...

In my humble opinion, "the anointing is that special endowment of power from on high, which helps us to accomplish through his Spirit, what we could not accomplish in our flesh."

Can it not be available to the local churches collectively, as well as to each individual member and constituent of his church? There by producing the necessary elements to allow his spirit and anointing to create the unity in his body that is so greatly needed.

I knew that there had been a need for plurality of leadership, as well as the need for a team spirit. These would both become more and more in evidence as the church grows and expands in ministries.

Whether we speak of the "Pastoral Staff," "Support Staff," "Board of Deacons," "Board of Trustees," or the other areas of leadership within the body, it is not only necessary but also imperative that the ministries flow together in unity. In addition, it is absolutely necessary to understand what the Anointing means to the spiritual survival of the body of Christ.

Synergism as it applies to the body of Christ... placing abilities in individuals that find they are able to work together in harmony. This will result in being more powerful working together as a team, or as a whole, rather than becoming separate entities.

In Phil. 2: 1-5 we read;

1 If you have any encouragement from being united with Christ, if any comfort from his love, if any fellowship with the Spirit, if any tenderness and compassion, 2 Then make my joy complete by being like-minded, having the same love, being one in spirit and purpose. 3 Do nothing out of selfish ambition or vain conceit, but in humility consider others better than yourselves. 4 Each of you should look not only to your own interests, but also to the interests of others. 5 Your attitude should be the same as that of Christ Jesus: NIV

In John 17, listen to the prayer of Jesus in the garden as he prays about the most important thing during and at the end of his earthly life, it was for his church, and for you and me.

John 17:20-23 (NIV)

20 "My prayer is not for them alone. I pray also for those who will believe in me through their message, 21 that all of them may be one, Father, just as you are in me and I am in you. May they also be in us so that the world may believe that you have sent me. 22 I have given them the glory that you gave me, that they may be one as we are one: 23 I in them and you in me. May they be brought to complete unity to let the world know that you sent me and have loved them even as you have loved me. Selah (AWESOME)

Teamwork Defined

The dictionary defines teamwork or a team as:

To harness or yoke together as a team; To join in a co-operative activity; Joint action by a group of people, in which each person; subordinates his individual interests and opinions to the unity and efficiency of the group. It was a coordinated effort, as of an athletic team. That is, A team of horses, harnessed to the same vehicle or plow and using their combined weight, to pull it.

Might that not also apply to a "team" of ministers or a leadership team, with Him being the captain?

Matthew's gospel, 11:28-30 really relates to this.

28 "Come to me, all you who are weary and burdened, and I will give you rest. 29 Take my yoke upon you and learn from me, for I am gentle and humble in heart, and you will find rest for your souls. 30 For my yoke is easy and my burden is light." (NIV)

When ministries and leadership become part of a team, they scripturally become fellow workers, together.

Col 4:11

Jesus, who is called Justus, also sends greetings. These are the only Jews among my fellow workers for the kingdom of God, and they have proved a comfort to me. (NIV)

They were also called fellow soldiers.

Phil 2:25

But I think it is necessary to send back to you Epaphroditus, my brother, fellow worker and fellow soldier, who is also your messenger, whom you sent to take care of my needs. (NIV)

Further, they were fellow servants.

Col 1:7-8

You learned it from Epaphras, our dear fellow servant, who is a faithful minister of Christ on our behalf, 8 and who also told us of your love in the Spirit. (NIV)

And also, fellow laborers.

Phil 4:3 Yes, and I ask you, loyal yokefellow, help these women who have contended at my side in the cause of the gospel, along with Clement and the rest of my fellow workers, whose names are in the book of life. (NIV)

Along with Fellow Helpers.

2 Cor 8:23

As for Titus, he is my partner and fellow worker among you; as for our brothers, they are representatives of the churches and an honor to Christ. (NIV)

Fellow Disciples.

John 11:16

Then Thomas (called Didymus) said to the rest of the disciples, "Let us also go, that we may die with him." (NIV)

Fellow Citizens.

Eph 2:19

Consequently, you are no longer foreigners and aliens, but fellow citizens with God's people and members of God's household, (NIV)

Fellow Heirs.

Eph 3:6 This mystery is that through the gospel the Gentiles are heirs together with Israel, members together of one body, and sharers together in the promise in Christ Jesus. (NIV)

And most importantly in fellowship with each other. Koinonia was key, meaning deep, covenant.

Gal 2:9 James, Peter and John, those reputed to be pillars, gave me and Barnabas the right hand of fellowship when they recognized the grace given to me. They agreed that we should go to the Gentiles, and they to the Jews. (NIV)

1 John 1:3-7 (NIV)

3 We proclaim to you what we have seen and heard, so that you also may have fellowship with us. And our fellowship is with the Father and with his Son, Jesus Christ. 4 We write this to make our joy complete. 5 This is the message we have heard from him and declare to you: God is light; in him there is no darkness at all. 6 If we claim to have fellowship with him yet walk in the darkness, we lie and do not live by the truth. 7 But if we walk in the light, as he is in the light, we have fellowship with one another, and the blood of Jesus, his Son, purifies us from all sin.

Acts 2:42 They devoted themselves to the apostles' teaching and to the fellowship, to the breaking of bread and to prayer. (NIV)

Rom 16:26 To the only wise God be glory forever through Jesus Christ! Amen. (NIV)

2 Cor 4:1 Therefore, since through God's mercy we have this ministry, we do not lose heart.

2 Cor 4:7 But we have this treasure in jars of clay to show that this all-surpassing power is from God and not from us.

2 Cor 4:10   We always carry around in our body the death of Jesus, so that the life of Jesus may also be revealed in our body. (NIV)

When Paul the Apostle writes to the church at Philippi, he shares several burdens. One of them is especially for two ladies for whom he has the deepest respect but is saddened by the problem that appears to exist between them, and asks that it be resolved. This is supported by the fact that in his letter he records that he literally pleaded with both of them to agree with each other in the Lord.

Phil 4:2. (NIV)   I plead with Euodia and I plead with Syntyche to agree with each other in the Lord.

In a scriptural context then, let us agree that "a church team then can be a group of Christian people joining together for the following reasons having the same mind, speaking the same thing, and going in the same direction, for the same reasons."

Again, he makes what I would consider an emotional appeal to the brethren. (Do you find it strange that he appealed to them as Brothers?)

1 Cor 1:10 (NIV)

I appeal to you, brothers, in the name of our Lord Jesus Christ, that all of you agree with one another so that there may be no divisions among you and that you may be perfectly united in mind and thought.

Phil 1 (NIV)

If you have any encouragement from being united with Christ, if any comfort from his love, if any fellowship with the Spirit, if any tenderness and compassion, 2 then make my joy complete by being like-minded, having the same love, being one in spirit and purpose. 3 do nothing out of selfish ambition or vain conceit, but in humility consider others better than yourselves. 4 each of you should look not only to your own interests, but also to the interests of others. 5 your attitude should be the same as that of Christ Jesus:

Conclusion

Building a team is not easy to do, but essential in the life of the church. It has been said that there is no "I" in team…as believers we are to learn to defer to others, even seeing them as greater than ourselves. When you are part of a team, the work of the Lord progresses in peace and in unity with limited burnout.

Chapter 8

The Attitudes of Our Leadership

Are there scriptures regarding the attitudes of leadership to which we should be paying attention? We answer a resounding "yes." I hope these scriptures, and the brief commentary at the end of this brief chapter, will speak to you as a leader or future leader in the body of Christ.

> Matthew 20:28 Your attitude must be like my own, for I, the Messiah, did not come to be served, but to serve, and to give my life as a ransom for many." (TLB)

> Acts 3:19 Now change your mind and attitude to God and turn to him so he can cleanse away your sins and send you wonderful times of refreshment from the presence of the Lord (TLB)

> Romans 15:5 May God who gives patience, steadiness, and encouragement help you to live in complete harmony with each other-each with the attitude of Christ toward the other. (TLB)

> 1 Peter 4:1 Since Christ suffered and underwent pain, you must have the same attitude he did; you must be ready to suffer, too. For remember, when your body suffers, sin loses its power, (TLB)

> 1 John 4:3 If not, the message is not from God but from one who is against Christ, like the "Antichrist" you have heard about who Is going to come, and his attitude of enmity against Christ is already abroad in the world. (TLB)

> Rev 2:16 "Change your mind and attitude, or else I will come to you suddenly and fight against them with the sword of my mouth. (TLB)

> Rev 2:21 I gave her time to change her mind and attitude, but she refused. (TLB)

Rev 9:21 Neither did they change their mind and attitude about all their murders and witchcraft, their immorality and theft. (TLB)

Rev 16:9 Everyone was burned by this blast of heat, and they cursed the name of God who sent the plagues-they did not change their mind and attitude to give him glory. (TLB)

The attitude of a leader does make a difference. Of course, the greatest leader of all is Jesus Christ. His attitude towards the religious was one of distain. His attitude towards the weak and disenfranchised was love and acceptance. His attitude towards his team was a desire to share the same glory as he had with his Father. As leaders, we have to always check our attitude, and ensure that we are serving as leaders in a way to honor Christ in everything.

Carnal Attitudes and Godly Leadership

Presented here is the apostle Paul's answer to carnal attitudes toward godly leadership.

1 Thess 5:12-17 (TMB)

12 Live the way he wants you to live. And now, friends, we ask you to honor those leaders who work so hard for you, who have been given the responsibility of urging and guiding you along in your obedience. 13 Overwhelm them with appreciation and love! Get along among yourselves, each of you doing your part. 14 Our counsel is that you warn the freeloaders to get a move on. Gently encourage the stragglers, and reach out for the exhausted, pulling them to their feet. Be patient with each person, attentive to individual needs. 15 And be careful that when you get on each other's nerves you don't snap at each other. Look for the best in each other, and always do your best to bring it out. 16 Be cheerful no matter what; 17 Pray all the time;

As to our own attitudes, could we again remind ourselves that we are, by faith, claiming what the Apostle Paul claimed when he wrote the following to the church at Galatia?

Gal 2:20-21 (TMB)

20 Christ's life showed me how, and enabled me to do it. I identified myself completely with him. Indeed, I have been crucified with Christ. My ego is no longer central. It is no longer important that I appear righteous before you or have your good opinion, and I am no longer driven to impress God. Christ lives in me. The life you see me living is not "mine," but it is lived by faith in the Son of God, who loved me and gave himself for me. 21 I am not going to go back on that. Is it not clear to you that to go back to that old rule keeping, peer-pleasing religion would be an abandonment of everything personal and free in my relationship with God? I refuse to do that, to repudiate God's grace. If a living relationship with God could come by rule keeping, then Christ died unnecessarily.

He further wrote to the church at Philippi the dangers of not being humble or led by His Spirit.

Does this verse sound like legalism or is it really just part of sanctification? Your attitude should be the kind that was shown us by Jesus Christ,

Phil 2:3-5 (TMB)

3 Don't push your way to the front; don't sweet-talk your way to the top. Put yourself aside, and help others get ahead. 4 Don't be obsessed with getting your own advantage. Forget yourselves long enough to lend a helping hand. 5 Think of yourselves the way Christ Jesus thought of himself.

A godly attitude can be cultivated...we must make it a priority.

Chapter 9

Team Goals

In the light of the scriptures and using sports as an analogy, (as the apostles did), how necessary is it for a team to have the same goals?

In the beginning of some ministries, a pastor sometimes has to do everything. This includes some things that he may not like to do, or things he has never had to do before. In my younger years in the ministry, a saying that was very helpful to me was this, "sometimes the only place you can find a helping hand is at the end of your own arm." Learning to delegate responsibility does not include simply finding someone else to do the job(s) that you may not enjoy doing. It really involves finding a person, or persons, that are "gifted" or may become gifted, in the areas of need.

Let me take a moment to suggest to you something you might do now, or if not now, sometime in the future when it seems appropriate. In one church, we had a "Potential Membership class" that was scheduled to be 8 weeks long; it was generally taught during the Sunday school hour. I talked with the pastoral staff about adding the class entitled, "Finding our GIFT" for the four following four weeks to fill out the SS quarter.

Since I was pastoring a larger church at that time, our list of potential ministries was very long. The list included approximately 75 ministries. Depending on the size of your congregation, you might have that put in a form entitled "Finding Your Ministry" and have it available to pass out during the last Sunday of that the membership class. This allows them to check the areas that they may feel they may be gifted in, in light of the class they have just completed. It might be wise to have them choose several areas, perhaps choice 1, choice 2, and choice 3. Make sure they fill in all the necessary contact information that may be needed in the future for ministries that need additional help.

Picking up where we left off:

Once assigning the position, provide them with a "job description." Where needed provide them the appropriate training. (Also on THE CD see list of training for ministries plus over 750 pages of helps both in administrative and practical areas of need) Allow them the latitude to carry out the ministry that they have just been assigned.) [3]

It would be good to remember that one person, even though they may have gifts in the area of leadership, cannot operate independently from others. How this is handled is often indicative of how successful he/she will ultimately be in what they have been called to do. You will soon discover their true motive for applying for the work; is it a desire to serve, or is it the possibility of recognition? It will soon be evident that one person cannot do it all, and let me encourage you to show appreciation to those who have helped to make the success possible:

- One man cannot shepherd successfully a large flock of God.

- One man is limited in his ministry and gifts.

- One man may fail in wisdom, knowledge and judgment.

- One man will have difficulty in finding the mind of God for everything.

- One man limits potential growth.

- One man has no one to adjust or correct him.

- One man has no "checks and balances".

- One man may brake physically, mentally, emotionally or morally under pressure.

- One man without proper direction may become an autocrat, better known as a dictator.

---

[3] See CD titled, Your Office and Administrative Companion" for some 58 church related job descriptions from CHURCH ENRICHMENT MINISTRIES, INC.

A one man ministry to the exclusion of others is contrary to the revealed will of God in the scriptures. Even a cursory study of His word teaches plurality of leadership as well as promotes the thought of someone who is "first among equals."

In the Old Testament, there are many men and women whom the Lord used to carry out His plan and purpose on the earth.

The Jethro Principle

We need to remember that when God called Moses from the burning bush, he told him what to do; he was later to be corrected in his decisions by Jethro, his Father-in-law.

This, as is the hope of any team, is the effort to bring the team to success. Although, there are those whose job it seems is more important, and in some cases it may be. But just as in football and other sports, it takes a team effort to accomplish the goal of winning.

It is in reading about David, Moses, Joseph, Paul and Peter, etc, that we realize how much they needed to depend on others to accomplish what they had been called to do. While David's life was overshadowed by his failures, he continued to be blessed through his repentance, (Psalm 51) and his constant desire to please his Lord. (Psalm 23)

While he wasn't allowed to actually build the temple, David made preparations for the completion of the temple through his son, King Solomon. Without His administrative arrangements and the training of 24,000 Levites beforehand, the dedication of The Temple by King Solomon, and once dedicated, for it to become operational, would not have been possible.

There is no doubt that there were many who never knew the things that David did behind the scenes to assure that the Temple had all the organizational and planning work done. Yet it was all completed before Solomon had finished the actual construction of the Temple. The kind of project David envisioned was immense. To build the physical structure would be challenging enough, but David was not interested in building a non-functioning cathedral to his God.

Though it would not be built by him, David could still envision this temple as a functioning worship center for Israel. God's promise of expanded territorial boundaries and a reign of peace for Solomon implied that the nation would realize a significant population increase. It would be a human resource director's nightmare to enlist, train, and supervise the number of workers necessary to ensure that the nation's needs would be met. Thus, toward the end of his life, David began organizing his people to be certain that the necessary tasks would be accomplished in an orderly manner for generations to come. Many of the structures he set in place survived the Babylonian Captivity and remained through the time of Christ.

David began with the Levites. By the end of his reign he had twenty-four thousand Levites trained to work in the Temple, these he organized, along with the priest's descendants from Aaron, into divisions. They were given specific responsibilities to be fulfilled during their times of duty in the Temple. Then he organized the rest of the Levites to be responsible for the other areas of ministry.

One significant aspect of ministry in the Temple was worship in song. Those who were skilled in vocal and instrumental music were organized into ministry teams under selected worship leaders. This aspect of worship was close to David's heart, he wrote over seventy psalms that were used in Temple worship. Many of those who led the worship teams were also among those who contributed to the recorded Psalms, including Asaph, Jeduthun and Heman.

No detail was overlooked in the preparation of the building that would house the worship of God. Some Levites were trained in and assigned to gate-keeping duties in both the Temple and the city. While some might view this position as insignificant, these men were responsible for crowd control and traffic flow to make certain that the worship of God would be conducted in an orderly manner, especially when large crowds arrived in Jerusalem for the feasts. Still others were assigned responsibilities in the treasuries, ensuring that the finances of the Temple were also managed well. Though much of David's interest focused on organizing the Temple staff, he also reorganized his military and political staff for greater efficiency.

Although Solomon's reign was to be characterized by peace, it would have been irresponsible for Israel to disband its armed forces. Knowing he had greater insight into human character than his young son, David placed men whom he considered reliable in various positions of responsibility throughout the kingdom. This would give Solomon time to concentrate on ruling the kingdom in the early days of his reign, knowing he could depend on those whom his father had placed in positions of influence.

Passing On Dreams to the Next Generation

With everything in place to ensure a smooth transition of power, David took time to challenge Solomon and others in prominent positions throughout the kingdom to pass on his dream to the next generation. He gathered leaders of the kingdom together in a solemn assembly, in order to share with them his vision. He reminded them of how it had been his desire to build the Temple, but God had said, "NO." He went on to explain how God had chosen Solomon to reign as his successor and to build His Temple.

As much as David wanted to talk about the Temple, he knew there was no use building the Temple if the nation had lost its zeal for God.

1 Chron 28:8-10 (TLB)

8 Then David turned to Solomon and said: "Here before the leaders of Israel, the people of God, and in the sight of our God, I am instructing you to search out every commandment of the Lord so that you may continue to rule this good land and leave it to your children to rule forever. 9 Solomon, my son, get to know the God of your fathers. Worship and serve him with a clean heart and a willing mind, for the Lord sees every heart and understands and knows every thought. If you seek him, you will find him; but if you forsake him, he will permanently throw you aside. 10 So be very careful, for the Lord has chosen you to build his holy Temple. Be strong and do as he commands." 11 Then David gave Solomon the blueprint of the Temple and its surroundings-the treasuries, the upstairs rooms, the inside rooms, and the sanctuary for the place of mercy. 12 He also gave Solomon his plans for

the outer court, the outside rooms, the Temple storage areas, and the treasuries for the gifts dedicated by famous persons. For the Holy Spirit had given David all these plans. 13 The king also passed on to Solomon the instructions concerning the work of the various groups of priests and Levites; and he gave specifications for each item in the Temple which was to be used for worship and sacrifice. 14 David weighed out enough gold and silver to make these various items, 15 as well as the specific amount of gold needed for the lamp stands and lamps. He also weighed out enough silver for the silver candlesticks and lamps, each according to its use. 16 He weighed out the gold for the table on which the Bread of the Presence would be placed and for the other gold tables, and he weighed the silver for the silver tables. 17 Then he weighed out the gold for the solid gold hooks used in handling the sacrificial meat and for the basins, cups, and bowls of gold and silver. 18 Finally, he weighed out the refined gold for the altar of incense and for the gold angels whose wings were stretched over the Ark of the Covenant of the Lord. 19 "Every part of this blueprint," David told Solomon, "was given to me in writing from the hand of the Lord." 20 Then he continued, "Be strong and courageous and get to work. Don't be frightened by the size of the task, for the Lord my God is with you; he will not forsake you. He will see to it that everything is finished correctly. 21 And these various groups of priests and Levites will serve in the Temple. Others with skills of every kind will volunteer, and the army and the entire nation are at your command."

Not even David was capable of doing ALL he wanted to do...he needed many, many skilled workers...following the pattern of Moses before him.

Chapter 10

The Call and Ministry of Moses

Even Moses, who we might say had really begun as a basket case, was the one who had the special experience of seeing the burning bush; and is, in fact, the one who received the call to leadership. Yet even with all that experience, he needed help and direction from, of all people, his father-in-law, Jethro.

It isn't recorded that Jethro experienced a burning bush as Moses did, but while Moses had been called to be God's man in leadership and was told what to do, he still had to "learn how" to get it done without exhaustion, or spiritual fatigue.

It was through the advice and counsel of Jethro, that he then began to learn about the plurality of leadership. It is better known in today's terms as a "team effort" and what we now know to be termed as "the importance of spiritual synergism." Let's take a quick look at that particular time in the life of Moses.....

> Ex 18:1 (NIV) Now Jethro, the priest of Midian and father-in-law of Moses, heard of everything God had done for Moses and for his people Israel, and how the LORD had brought Israel out of Egypt.

> Ex 18:13-16 (NIV) 13 The next day Moses took his seat to serve as judge for the people, and they stood around him from morning till evening. 14 When his father-in-law saw all that Moses was doing for the people, he said, "what is this you are doing for the people? why do you alone sit as judge, while all these people stand around you from morning till evening?" 15 Moses answered him, "Because the people come to me to seek God's will. 16 Whenever they have a dispute, it is brought to me, and I decide between the parties and inform them of god's decrees and laws."

> Ex 18:17-26 (NIV)

17 Moses' father-in-law replied, "what you are doing is not good! (Please note) Wow! What preacher is going to take that from his father-in-law, or from anyone else for that matter? After all, he's the one that was spoken to, or called to leadership, out of the burning bush, not Jethro! And yet it was Jethro, who he continued to let him know that he was not going to be able to continue on like he was doing it) 18 You and these people who come to you will only wear yourselves out. The work is too heavy for you; you cannot handle it alone. 19 Listen now to me (are we in a place right now, or when needed, to listen to others? hear him) and I will give you some advice, and may God be with you. You must be the people's representative before God and bring their disputes to him. 20 Teach them the decrees and laws, and show them the way to live and the duties they are to perform. (Wouldn't that at least sound like a job description?) 21 But select capable men from all the people--men who fear God, trustworthy men who hate dishonest gain--and appoint them as officials over thousands, hundreds, fifties and tens. (Is the amount of people for which we have responsibility really important to us? Are we at times discouraged by the few that are in attendance? Or are we concerned about the size and place and the people where we are? Be it 10, 50, or 1000?) 22 Have them serve as judges for the people at all times, but have them bring every difficult case to you; the simple cases they can decide themselves. That will make your load lighter, because they will share it with you. 23 if you do this and god so commands, you will be able to stand the strain, and all these people will go home satisfied." 24 Moses listened to his father-in-law and did everything he said. 25 He chose capable men from all Israel and made them leaders of the people, officials over thousands, hundreds, fifties and tens. 26 They served as judges for the people at all times. The difficult cases they brought to Moses, but the simple ones they decided themselves. (NIV)

Please note: there is a real need for sharing information with the senior pastor. Many times he may already be aware of the need, and it might help him to deal with the issues behind the scenes that may be known by only a few.

Not just anyone could serve in a leadership capacity; there were very important qualifications for leadership. They had to be able men, men who fear God, men of truth, men hating covetousness, men of wisdom, Knowledge (the possession of the facts), understanding (the interpretation of the facts), and wisdom (the application of the facts). Further, they had to be people who could take responsibility as those to be chosen, with the ability to rule their own spirit well and rule their own house. If these two be done, then, they would be eligible to rule in the house of God.

Moses, under the advice of Jethro, placed as heads to rule over the thousands, hundreds, fifties, and tens, as they were gifted men, able to judge the people at all times able to:

- judge with mercy
- judge with grace & compassion
- judge with humility
- judge with justice
- judge without partiality
- judge beyond natural senses
- judge with knowledge, understanding and wisdom
- judge after having all of the available facts.

They were men that would help bear the burden with Moses, men having the same spirit on them, and thus able to assist in the great responsibility of Moses, so he could maintain his relationship with both God and his fellow man.

When all is said and done, the measure of ability is the measure of responsibility, which becomes the measure of authority and the measure of one's accountability. One only has authority when they have responsibility.

Then Jethro's ministry became, in reality, a team ministry (a team that later would be problematic for Moses, thus leading to the need for elders carrying his heart, see Numbers 11:16-17)

> 1 Cor 2:14 (TLB) 14 But the man who isn't a Christian can't understand and can't accept these thoughts from God, which the Holy Spirit teaches us. They sound foolish to him because only those who have the Holy Spirit within them can understand what the Holy Spirit means. Others just can't take it in!

Chapter 11

Accountability

Authority and responsibility without accountability can create a serious problem. In almost all evangelical churches, spiritual authority and administrative authority are given to the Senior Pastor. It is also designated to church leadership, but that authority, spiritual or administrative, was never intended to be abused!

No doubt you are aware that some major church organizations have adopted a doctrine which applies to some of the designated leaders. In some ways it negates the responsibility of those who are in a lesser position of leadership by use of the term, ex-cathedra, meaning that to hear them verbally or in writing, is to hear from God Himself.

This is considered by most to be a dangerous as well as a destructive, and a divisive doctrinal position. It has been, especially in the last several hundred years, a source of great disputation. No one has the right to claim equality with God, or to speak for God, unless by the gift of the Holy Spirit; even then there are those that can judge what has been said in the light of the scriptures. Regardless of how spiritual they may appear to be, some have made this mistake; it is a mistake that the devil himself made as recorded in Isaiah 14. It's the "I will" factor!

Isa 14:12-17 (TLB)

12 How you are fallen from heaven, O Lucifer, son of the morning! How you are cut down to the ground-mighty though you were against the nations of the world. 13 For you said to yourself, (As a man thinks in his heart). "I will ascend to heaven and rule the angels. I will take the highest throne. I will preside on the Mount of Assembly far away in the north. 14 I will climb to the highest heavens and be like the Most High." 15 But instead, you will be brought down to the pit of hell, down to its lowest depths. 16 Everyone there will stare at you and ask, "Can this be the one who shook the

earth and the kingdoms of the world? 17 Can this be the one who destroyed the world and made it into a shambles, who demolished its greatest cities and had no mercy on his prisoners?"

Our authority was and is still given to us to be used for His glory only, and not for our own personal agenda or financial gain. There are, however, in some extreme situations, members of congregations that are just so taken with the personalities that they are willing to overlook even known and practiced sin, in order to placate a particular minister and keep him at their church.

Here is a verse we previously used; we include it again for remembrance sake.

> 24 Remember that some men, even pastors, lead sinful lives, and everyone knows it. In such situations you can do something about it. But in other cases only the judgment day will reveal the terrible truth. 25 In the same way, everyone knows how much good some pastors do, but sometimes their good deeds aren't known until long afterward.

When the analogy of faith (comparing scripture with scripture) is not balanced by both the context and other supporting scriptures, we are at times in danger of using verses of scripture to support what we want it to say or do, on our own behalf.

In the book of Romans, 13:1, the apostle Paul makes clear what he is teaching about authority, especially when it involves character and reputation.

> Rom 13:1-5 (TLB)

> 1 Obey the government, (It is implied in other scriptures that obedience to government authority is required until or unless it is in direct conflict with His word) for God is the one who has put it there. There is no government anywhere that God has not allowed to be placed in power. 2 So those who refuse to obey the laws of the land are refusing to obey God, and punishment will follow. 3 For the policeman does not frighten people who are doing right; but those doing evil

will always fear him. So if you don't want to be afraid, keep the laws and you will get along well. 4 The policeman is sent by God to help you. But if you are doing something wrong, of course you should be afraid, for he will have you punished. God sends him for that very purpose. 5 Obey the laws, then, for two reasons: first, to keep from being punished, and second, just because you know you should.

Chapter 12

Letters of Interest

The contents of this letter (used by permission), and the ones to follow, are from a very concerned church member.

The letter should give us reason to pause, and where and when possible, to sound an alarm about arrogance and divisiveness, especially among, but not limited to, the smaller growing churches,

Even in the early church, they had to warn all believers about the possibility of divisiveness caused by lack of unity in and among those professing to be Christians. Let us take heed to the three years of warnings, and what he was warning about.

ACTS 20:17-31 (NIV)

17 From Miletus, Paul sent to Ephesus for the elders of the church. 18 When they arrived, he said to them: "You know how I lived the whole time I was with you, from the first day I came into the province of Asia. 19 I served the Lord with great humility and with tears, although I was severely tested by the plots of the Jews. 20 You know that I have not hesitated to preach anything that would be helpful to you but have taught you publicly and from house to house. 21 I have declared to both Jews and Greeks that they must turn to God in repentance and have faith in our Lord Jesus. 22 "And now, compelled by the Spirit, I am going to Jerusalem, not knowing what will happen to me there. 23 I only know that in every city the Holy Spirit warns me that prison and hardships are facing me. 24 However, I consider my life worth nothing to me, if only I may finish the race and complete the task the Lord Jesus has given me — the task of testifying to the gospel of God's grace. 25 "Now I know that none of you among whom I have gone about preaching the kingdom will ever see me again. 26 Therefore, I declare to you today that I am innocent of the blood of all men. 27

For I have not hesitated to proclaim to you the whole will of God. 28 Keep watch over yourselves and all the flock of which the Holy Spirit has made you overseers. Be shepherds of the church of God, which he bought with his own blood.

Following are some of the most powerful words in the whole New Testament, both the (NIV) & (KJV). The apostle Paul warned the church with tears for three years. About those that would not spare the flock, but will distort the truth, and draw away disciples after themselves.

29 I know that after I leave, savage wolves will come in among you and will not spare the flock. 30 Even from your own number men will arise and distort (disfigure, twist, and warp) the truth in order to draw away disciples after them. 31 So be on your guard! Remember that for three years I never stopped warning each of you night and day with tears. (NIV)

Now from the King James for special emphasis.

29 For I know this, that after my departing shall grievous wolves enter in among you, not sparing the flock. 30 Also of your own selves shall men arise, speaking perverse things, to draw away disciples after them. 31 Therefore watch, and remember, that by the space of three years I ceased not to warn every one night and day with tears.

The following was written in letterform, by a church member, having just experienced a serious conflict caused by a challenge for leadership that had arisen in the church to which she had become a member. She felt it necessary to write this article describing, to the best of her ability, the cause and effect of those who would not only seek to be in control, but unfortunately in their endeavor to be successful in their desire to win, they would continue their divisive and destructive attacks, this is in spite of the consequences to the Gospel, The ultimate damage to new converts, Including those veterans of past church conflicts that may be "wounded in action"

The effect of the fallout may hinder the spiritual growth and development of weaker Christians who may become a casualty as the result of a dysfunctional conflict. Without regard to the disorderliness it may cause His body, known as the church. To say nothing of the damage to his name and his character that he has used to redeem us.

I am sure that those of us who abhor such a divisive spirit would want to appeal to churches and Para-church organization in other places, to be aware. If we do not keep the anointing on our lives, and rebuke the evil spirit of divisiveness, that irreparable damage can be done to those who have put their trust and faith in God, but are looking to what they hope is spiritual leadership for their own spiritual growth and development.

During board or business meetings, if we do not continually reaffirm the unity that continually reminds us that it is not about us, discord will always be at the center. It is in fact about our Lord and Savior, Jesus Christ, who continually, through his word, expresses his desire that others may be won by having his love and Holy Spirit continue to be seen through the lives of those he has redeemed. After Pentecost they almost immediately continued in fellowship by joining together in the breaking of bread, and praising God.

Acts 2:46-47 (NIV)

46 "Every day they continued to meet together in the temple courts. They broke bread in their homes and ate together with glad and sincere hearts, 47 praising God and enjoying the favor of all the people. And the Lord added to their number daily those who were being saved."

It should be said here that not all churches or Para-church organizations are faced with the severity of the "control" problem as others may face. While the events in the following scene were real, it is written with a desire to admonish us all that we need to, if at all possible, avoid church controversy that all too often results in a "split" or dissolution of that particular body of believers. It is also, in all too many cases, does irreparable damage to both the new and older converts alike. We must, as the scriptures enjoin us, "Live peaceably with all men".

Please remember that while there was no little problem between Paul and Barnabus, the controversy that existed between them, while it did end in them going in different directions, was not based on personal gain, of the desire to be in control. It must be understood that in Paul's opinion, the Gospel would be hurt if John Mark would defect again while working on the field as a missionary. In my humble opinion, the difference was really based upon the following.

Paul was defending the Church as an Apostle, Barnabus, whose name meant, "Son of Consolation", was concerned about the person of John Mark, and while endeavoring to defend him, as the name Barnabus would reflect, took issue to the Apostle Paul. This, Barnabus, was the very same person that Paul had stood up for when, after his salvation, the church in Jerusalem would not, because of fear and trepidation, let Paul join the church.

1 Thess 5:11-13 (TLB)

11 So encourage each other to build each other up, just as you are already doing. 12 Dear brothers, honor the officers of your church who work hard among you and warn you against all that is wrong. Think highly of them and give them your wholehearted love because they are straining to help you. And remember, no quarreling among yourselves. 13 Show them great respect and wholehearted love because of their work. And live peacefully with each other.

May you or your church never have to personally endure the following account of "the casualties of a church in conflict" continuing to be described by the following:

To the occasional visitor, nothing may even be suspicious.

It was membership Sunday at our church, and the class looked so nice as they accepted their certificates of membership. The senior pastor & his wife, followed by each associate pastor and then the board members and their wives, ceremoniously passed by and welcomed them as the congregation applauded. I fidgeted with the neckline of my dress and prayed that the cease-fire would last.

We were really a church at war. There were two very recognizable factions within the church – each representing a very vocal minority group –but the numbers were growing with sides vying for control.

There had been several heartless altercations but for months now, the fields of battle had been silent. With each passing day we were tempted to breathe a sigh of relief. Still some questions had to be answered.

Had forgiveness and unity gone beyond the conference table and into the hearts? Was the conflict really over? Or was the silence only because the other side was involved in the developing of a spiritual tidal wave, known in the Far East as a tsunami. This unseen enemy could just about destroy everything in its path. Many individuals, (see picture of an actual tsunami and the horror on the faces of those realizing that in a matter of minutes, many of them may die), having no idea of the magnitude of this storm, these victims were not able to escape the deluge of the storm, nor are those that are caught in the middle of a meeting where anger, unkindness, antagonism, and resentment was about to be poured out on that congregation. Unfortunately, as with the tsunami, many would never fully recover.

Using this analogy, could this not be the description of the destructive condition in the church that the Apostle John was writing about in 3rd John? Isn't the conflict as described by John pretty close to being an overwhelming challenge for the early church as well as for us today?

3 John 9-11 (NIV)

9 I wrote to the church, but Diotrephes, who loves to be first, will have nothing to do with us. 10 So if I come, I will call attention to what he is doing, gossiping maliciously about us. Not satisfied with that, he refuses to welcome the brothers. He also stops those who want to do so and puts them out of the church. 11 Dear Friend, do not imitate what is evil but what is good. Anyone who does what is good is from God. Anyone who does what is evil has not seen God.

I am sure that the following words have been experienced over and over again in congregations that have allowed members or constituents to continue to live in an attitude of bitterness and anger, that has had, or is now having, a direct affect on other important areas of ministry and in many cases, due to the fall out of such contention over power and control, the reputation of the church has been destroyed, in many cases at least hindered, to the extent that no further work based on Christianity of any magnitude would be possible for some years to come, or be accomplished where conflict has become known through individuals or the news media.

The Apostle John is letting the church know that this kind of attitude cannot be tolerated, and he will deal with it when he arrives. Because of the consequences that are often the result of outward conflict, the apostle gives an assurance that he is going to deal with this entire situation when he comes.

It is important that I mention at this juncture that when you enter into this realm of spiritual battle, that we are not fighting with the ability of flesh and blood, but in the demonstration of the spirit, power and a sound mind. Our intention is to bring healing, not further rumblings or disagreements, adding to the already difficult circumstances.

3 John 9-11 (TLB).

9 I sent a brief letter to the church about this, but proud Diotrephes, who loves to push himself forward as the leader of the Christians there, does not admit my authority over him and refuses to listen to me. (How destructive and divisive is that?) 10 When I come I will tell you some of the things he is doing and what wicked things he is saying about me, the insulting language he is using. He not only refuses to welcome the missionary travelers himself but tells others not to, and when they do he tries to put them out of the church. 11 Dear Friend, don't let this bad example influence you. Follow only what is good. Remember that those who do what is right prove that they are God's children; and those who continue in evil prove that they are far from God

Unfortunately, there are those that, with otherwise tender spirits, may want nothing to do with any controversy. Their attitude is just having peace almost at any cost, no matter how destructive, and it will ultimately go away.

Just one other thought about this. Be careful, if you are one that would be involved in the handling of such situations. When correcting, it should only be attempted by those who are spiritually mature

John in his epistle, not only named the one whose attitude was affecting and infecting the entire church body, but that he would personally deal with it when he arrived. (When using names publically great wisdom must be sought)

Would you believe that there are those in some churches that have the attitude like the one to whom John was referring. Is it possible that narcissism (self love) had so enveloped him that he really believed that he was "God's special child" and that God had given him special permission to make major decisions in the church regardless of his poor attitude, or what those decisions may cost?

My good friend, Rev. J. M. Donahue of Louisville, KY, wrote a most telling poem about those who would presume to be among those who think more about themselves than they ought. They seem to live to be appreciated, and if not recognized sufficiently, they will quite often simply leave to find a place that will take notice of their talents and recognize how important they are.

It's Movin' Time Again

From church to church they go, with baggage in their hand
Somebody hurt his feelings, so it's movin' time again,
Off to find another church and a preacher who understands.
And will pacify his every whim, or it's movin' time again.

It's great to be a visitor everyone seemed so kind,
They treat you like an honored guest, and make you feel divine,
Hope they don't expect commitment, like some that I've been to,
Oh the burden of involvement, and the things they put you through.

It's Sunday school and Children's church, then its youth and teens,
Tithing and pledges, beats anything you've ever seen,
The preacher's sermons are too long; the choir's way too loud,
They better get their act together, or I'll not join that crowd.

Man, have they got a hang-up, all they preach about is sin,
If that's the way it's going to be, then it's movin' time again,
"Now I've tried to be a blessing, the Lord knows my heart is true,
But I see so many of their sins, it hurts me through and through."

When accused of being a gossip, they said, "I'd have to see the board,"
I just told that church to forget it, I was going to serve my Lord,
And no one has a right to correct me, or they'll get a piece of my mind,
Jesus and me have our own thing going, and that just suits me fine.

Some Churches don't know the value, of having me attend,
And if this church don't line up with me, it's movin' time again.
Somewhere in this city, there is a church just waiting for me,
Where I can display my talents, for the Christian world to see,

Where good friends will be there for me, and never let me down,
They will thank God for His blessing, of just havin' me around,
And Lord knows that I am special, His child, redeemed from sin,
If they don't appreciate me there, then it will be movin' time again.

J. M. Donahue, Louisville, KY 1990

How unbearably true!

I guess we need to be reminded occasionally that In the Old Testament, Nehemiah, sent by the King to rebuild the walls of Jerusalem, not only had to deal with attacks from outside the walls, but continually had to deal with those inside the walls. These were his own people that were constantly at war with him over something.

Neh 2:17-20 (KJV)

17 Then said I unto them, Ye see the distress that we are in, how Jerusalem lieth waste, and the gates thereof are burned with fire: come, and let us build up the wall of Jerusalem, that we be no more a reproach. 18 Then I told them of the hand of my God which was good upon me; as also the king's words that he had spoken unto me. And they said, Let us rise up and build. So they strengthened their hands for this good work. 19 But when Sanballat the Horonite, and Tobiah the servant, the Ammonite, and Geshem the Arabian, heard it, they laughed us to scorn, and despised us, and said, what is this thing that ye do? Will ye rebel against the king? 20 Then answered I them, and said unto them, The God of heaven, he will prosper us; therefore we his servants will

arise and build: but ye have no portion, nor right, nor memorial, in Jerusalem.

Human nature has not changed much. This nature of ours, unless there is a spiritual "heart transplant", has remained the same since the fall of Adam and Eve.

More Letters

When these wars occur, they are much like the war in America that raged on during the 1860s. Each side, north and south sent their Christian sons, some from the same families, to the battlefronts on opposite sides.

Issues divided a nation into two sides, each side convinced that God would champion their cause. Believing this, they took up weapons and murdered, maimed, or left for dead their fellow countrymen, believers and unbelievers alike.

I am stunned by what professing Christians will do and say, one against another, supposing in the name of Lord. I read an article that shared how the first two rows of ministers at a denominational conference protested women preachers by standing up and turning their backs towards the speaker, Anne Graham Lotz.

At what point does the fight become so furious that we lose sight of the two most important commandments?

"Love the lord your God with all of your heart, mind and soul, and love your neighbor as yourself."

Have you ever asked yourself or some of the combatants what they think happens to love and kindness when battle lines are established in a church setting?"

One of the answers puts the blame squarely on the shoulders of our mutual enemy who often uses those wearing the same uniform to attack, especially the under-shepherds that are being used in the ministry, as well as wounding others that are involved in the leadership of the body of Christ.

> Zech 13:6 (NIV) 6 If someone asks him, 'What are these wounds on your body?' he will answer, 'The wounds I was given at the house of my friends.'

It is evident from the Scriptures that everything that is said with unkindness or malice, without repentance, will be dealt with at the judgment. There are those, I am sure that have no idea how serious our Lord is about our actions and attitudes. How serious do you think Jesus is when making these accusations while discussing this particular subject?

> Matt 12:34-37 (TLB)

> 34 You brood of snakes! How could evil men like you speak what is good and right? For a man's heart determines his speech. 35 A good man's speech reveals the rich treasures within him. An evil-hearted man is filled with venom, and his speech reveals it. 36 And I tell you this, that you must give account on judgment day for every idle word you speak. 37 your words now reflect your fate then: either you will be justified by them or you will be condemned."

In the Old Testament, we read about the condition of our hearts in relation to our words that we speak, including those thoughts that we don't express verbally, but think them in our minds and hearts. We need to pay attention to the state of our hearts, when we speak or are encouraged by circumstances, or to even think unkind thoughts.

> Ps 19:14 (NIV) 14 May the words of my mouth and the meditation of my heart (includes what we are thinking) be pleasing in your sight, O LORD, my Rock and my Redeemer.

A bit of commentary will help clarify this concept.

There is no way of knowing or measuring the effects of division or conflict, it could last for years to come. The New Testament writer James was convinced our faith should not just be in word, but also in deed. In the first chapter, verses nineteen and twenty he writes: "My dear brothers, take note of this: Everyone should be quick to listen and slow to become angry, for man's anger does not bring about the righteous life that God desires."

There are numerous battles occurring both within and between churches. Well-meaning Christians, so impassioned with their "cause," often fail to consider God's will, according to his plan and purpose. Derailed by the heat of the battle, many lose their ability to discern the difference between what is flesh and what is God.

There is no way of knowing the amount of damage that can or has been done by the actions of those who have allowed a carnal spirit to dominate their words and actions. Those that have been affected or infected by their attitudes have all too often ended up being AWOL from God's Army.

I am sure that no one really knows the amount of churches, ministers, and/or church leaders, whose ministries have been brought to a bitter end by those putting their personal agendas in place of God's plan and purpose.

There are no doubt many, whose wounds have left them spiritually crippled for the rest of their lives. What I have covered in Chapter 8 of 1 Corinthians, and Chapter 14 of Romans, deals directly with The Apostle Paul's efforts to straighten out the 9 or more problems described in his epistle to the Corinthian Church. Among them are the challenges that come from those who don't really seem to care about what anyone else thinks or how they may be affected or infected by their attitude, actions, and/or use of words.

For too long, members and attendees, especially of some Evangelical Churches have been allowed, without appropriate correction or exhortation, to say, act, and in some cases, even make and express unfair personal opinions and judgments of those who they may not like, or even care about. I have seen smaller churches become even smaller, as the years pass by. Splitting and then splitting again over personal preferences, authority, and control, while some even display their childish actions.

Paul mentions this while dealing with the law of love in His first letter to the Corinthians.

1 Cor 3:1-8 (KJV)

1 And I, brethren, could not speak unto you as unto spiritual, but as unto carnal, even as unto babes in Christ. 2 I have fed you with milk, and not with meat: for hitherto ye were not able to bear it, neither yet now are ye able. 3 For ye are yet carnal: for whereas there is among you envying, and strife, and divisions, are ye not carnal, and walk as men? 4 For while one saith, I am of Paul; and another, I am of Apollos; are ye not carnal? 5 Who then is Paul, and who is Apollos, but ministers by whom ye believed, even as the Lord gave to every man?

6 I have planted, Apollos watered; but God gave the increase. 7 So then neither is he that planteth anything, neither he that watereth; but God that giveth the increase. 8 Now he that planteth and he that watereth are one: and every man shall receive his own reward according to his own labour. 1 Cor 13:11 (KJV) When I was a child , I spake as a child , I understood as a child, I thought as a child : but when I became a man, I put away childish things.

How often in church during board meetings, and/or business meetings, (especially among those to have been elected to leadership, because of their years of service) do those who have professed to being Christians for years and years, still fight and fume over the smallest of matters. Majoring in minors, and treating things that didn't really matter, as if they are of major importance.

In my research, I have found that there are seven areas of vulnerability for those in spiritual leadership. One of the key areas of vulnerability comes from wounds and offenses, where leaders allow their feelings to be hurt quickly and often. It is hard to help them get victory over the situation since they feel that someone one else is responsible for their dilemma. Yet in many cases, it's their own "spiritual immaturity" that is the cause for being (using God's army as a metaphor) "wounded in action."

Another Poignant Letter

Here is another letter written to a church board expressing concern about the treatment of their pastor. Many times they will leave one church and bring that same spirit of over-sensitivity right along with them, infecting and affecting anyone that comes in contact with their divisive attitude. When new members apply for church membership, they should be questioned by the church which they are now attending. In addition, contacting the pastor or board from the church they just left may help to resolve old issues and derail new problems from developing in the future.

As we mentioned at the beginning of this book, there are several layers of responsibility. Certainly there is enough to go around when it comes to church control, or those that would seek positions to control. Good control is necessary. Those that are selfish, self-willed, untrained and unqualified, especially those that want to impose their personal convictions or worse yet "their rules" of conduct and appearance, may lack a basic education, or harbor a bad attitude. This affects and can potentially infect just about everything; and in some cases, everyone that comes in contact with them.

I listed at the top, the Sr. Pastor which can, by his deportment and attitude, be a blessing or in other cases, somewhat of a challenge to listen to. In addition, I mentioned several other areas, one of which was the congregation at large, but also the elected or appointed boards. There are of course, depending on the church, boards called by different names.

Board of deacons was the most popular for a long time. Then in addition, some churches had a board of elders, a trustee board, or maybe in a smaller setting a board of advisors made up of just a few dependable people you could trust.

This next letter involves some problems with some board members who took ownership and charge of all major decisions that had to do with that church. As a result, one man that served on the board must have had his eye anointed with eye salve. He, through the following letter that he had written with the deepest sense of humility and concern, challenged the very attitudes about which the Apostle Paul and other leaders of the early church dealt with so adamantly.

Please read this carefully and with the deepest sense of love and gratitude for God's grace and mercy. This is not being published to embarrass anyone, but to, as much as lieth within us, fulfill the concerns of our Lord that he prayed in the Garden recorded in the 17th Chapter of the book of John. His chief concern was his followers, that his church might become one as he was one with his Father and the Holy Spirit.

Might I suggest to you, when and if you have time to open your Bible to the 17th Chapter of John, and after reading the whole chapter verse by verse, that you re-read it one verse at a time, and that you become your own commentator. After each verse, write or type what you feel He is saying about His church in relationship to the world. Seventeen times He mentions the world system, during His prayer, (17 times). It may open up a whole new frame of reference by the time you were finished with your own commentary.

This was another letter that had been given to me that made me realized how important our treatment of each other is, including the Sr. Pastor. His scriptural position should be honored and he should be held in high esteem, especially if we are professing to be a man or woman in whom His Spirit dwells.

To quote an advertisement from one of the newer drinks given to us for more energy, apply it's analogy to our being filled with His Spirit. "Is it in you"? As you read this, how about quoting it this way, Is (the Holy Spirit) in you?

In this letter, a board member reaches out, apparently having the Holy Spirit's insight in revealing the basic problems that may exist in all too many churches. I have traveled much, and observed much, and have seen maybe too much. This letter hits at the very core of the problems many churches are facing when it comes to having to deal with those that leave no question about their wanting control. They make sure that in each meeting, either together or in small groups, their message is clear.

The following is not to bring justification to undeserving leadership, be it pastor, board, staff, committee, or any other area of leadership. There are generally 3 positions that evolve out of confrontation.

1. When the pastor is set on having his own way and only giving others that disagree the choice of his way or the highway.

2. When the board or staff decides that their way is better contrary to the good job being done by the senior pastor.

3. When a person, group, family or wealthy leaders, use their longevity, and sometimes even their financial status, to decide that the church and all that is in it really belongs to them. They then are no longer just stewards, but in addition, they insist on controlling everything as well.

Be it a pastor or board, pastoral or support staff, this sets the stage for a continual battle for control that often results in conflict.

Another brother writes to discuss several leadership positions, the first:

To board members and pastors everywhere,

Please indulge me for a few minutes to express some thoughts that have been on my heart concerning our Pastor/ Board relationship and specifically the review process that we have been involved in these past few months. I believe that our inability to bring this process to conclusion now after the third meeting on the issue is, quite frankly, to our shame and definitely not to our credit. This, in itself, can only lead the Pastor to believe that either we are in serious disagreement, or that we have great contentions about his ability to lead this church. I suspect that for some members of the board, the latter, IS an accurate conclusion.

There is a decided difference between bringing short comings to a pastor's attention to further strengthen this church body by encouraging him to make adjustments, rather than making an itemized list of all the singular things he's supposed to have done that someone may disagree with. There appears to be a spirit of accusation present at our review meetings and generally at most board meetings of late. It's almost as if certain individuals are watching for the opportunity to oppose or disagree. There does not appear to be a spirit of unity among the brothers, much less between the Board and Pastor.

I'm not sure I understand why, but this Board seems to operate at a confrontational level, one that I have difficulty dealing with. I'm not confrontational by nature; in fact, there's almost nothing that I dislike more. I find myself in a constant state of turmoil over board issues, and contrary to my understanding of how a room full of born-again; Spirit filled leaders should be interacting and responding to each other and their pastor, I'm finding myself actually grieved in my spirit as I anticipate the next meeting.

According to their own admission, many feel that conflict is good and brings resolution, and to a point, I agree. But, to the contrary, it seems that we are in constant turmoil, constantly at odds with each other and with Pastor. This to me is counter-productive as well as destructive, and will do nothing more than cause further division within the board and ultimately, throughout the church body.

Possibly, my perception is wrong, but I believe that some board members have completely lost their support of Pastor and can no longer be cooperative and supportive. If this cannot be re-established; if trust and faith in our Pastor as our spiritual leader at a board level is not reaffirmed, then we will continue to experience division and strife that will surely have its effect on the entire congregation.

I realize that we, as Board members, are responsible to review Pastor's performance each year and help him move in a direction toward improving the overall effectiveness and impact that his ministry has on our congregation. But I believe our present focus, for the most part, is lacking in forgiveness, lacking in loving correction, and instead is flavored with bitterness over what has perceived to have happened in the past.

Paul admonishes the believers at Ephesus with these words,

(Eph. 4:31-32)

"Let all bitterness, and wrath, and anger, and clamor, and evil speaking be put away from you be kind to one another, tenderhearted, forgiving one another, even as God for Christ's sake has forgiven you."

He was talking to Christians, church members, and leaders; because there was a problem in the church with these issues. I believe that we need to deal with issues as they arise, that we do not shrink from our responsibility as leaders to this body, but firmly believe that we, collectively as a board, need to put the past behind us, along with the bitterness, hurt, and anger, and now concentrate on being kind to one another, tenderhearted and forgiving, going on with what God has for this church now and in the future.

The writer of Hebrews (12: 14-15) instructs us to "make effort to live in peace with all men and to be holy; without holiness no one will see the Lord. See to it that no one misses the grace of God and that no bitter root grows up to cause trouble and defile many."

This applies to our relationship with "all men" but certainly and specifically to our relationship with each other as brothers and sisters in Christ and with our Pastor, our shepherd. We need to guard ourselves against any "root of bitterness" that may rise up, do not be so quick to find fault, but "make an effort to live in peace" as brothers and sisters in the Lord.

As we stand in review of a Pastor's performance, let's not forget that what he does, and does well in my opinion, is minister to this body. Pastor's preaching in the past few months has been powerful, inspired and effective, bringing many to our altars to respond positively to the spoken Word. He is much loved by the members and attendees of this body, finding in his preaching, a loving, caring and edifying ministry.

The Pastor presents himself with excellence at weddings and funerals, being extremely personal, sensitive and caring for our church body. Pastor expresses often from the pulpit and at a personal level, his desire to see the gifts of the Spirit in operation and a desire for a deeper, Spirit-filled worship in our services. His teaching has been excellent, well attended and with good response from the Body. Pastor is highly respected and loved throughout the community" even the secular community" and finds favor and honor throughout the nation and abroad.

In my opinion "we have much to be thankful for in our Pastor's years here and believe that he is a man able to handle constructive criticism" but if there are apparent weaknesses, we need to address these areas needing improvement in a more constructive manner.

Brothers, it is not my intention to bring fault or point the finger of accusation at anyone. Whenever there is conflict of any kind in my personal life, my nature is to look inwardly for the solution.

Are any of us perfect? Certainly not, and .I know that indeed, no pastor, while having gained experience, would agree with that statement concerning himself as well.

But can we consider and weigh the fact that everything we do in this boardroom should be bathed in prayer, kindness, soft hearts and forgiveness? These are all things that God's Word encourages and admonishes us to do in our relations in the world. How much more so in our relations with each other? Are we, collectively, as board members, perfect? Again the answer has to be, certainly not.

Have you not sensed the tension around this table at recent meetings? Has your spirit been grieved, as mine has, as we deliberate issues? Have we approached every issue prayerfully, humbly seeking God's counsel, putting everything at His feet in submission to His guidance and direction? I'm afraid the answer has to be no.

I think we need a serious change in attitude. I'm starting to question whether the enemy is trying to bring division and strife. Because if it was ordained of God to bring resolve and peace, then why are we always, meeting after meeting, in a state of turmoil?

Maybe part of the answer is to spend some time together off-site with pastor; not to accuse and blame, but to find unity and peace. But I truly believe that the unity and peace we seek needs to start right in our own prayer closets. The relationship between pastor and the board needs to be placed in the hands of the Lord. It cannot continue the way it is right now. There has to be healing, compassion and love inserted in order for God to continue His work in any church body. Peace and unity need to be restored; without it, no pastor will be able to continue an effective ministry if there is an attitude in leadership that demands "control" and will ultimately hinder those in leadership from effectively representing his body.

I appeal to you as my brothers in Christ, to carefully consider the pathway that God is taking us on, and to humbly submit ourselves to His guidance and direction.

May I make some observations concerning the review process? No one wants to be given all negatives in relation to their performance, on the job, or otherwise. I suggest that we be positive, fair, and honest in our assessment of what we feel Pastor is doing well, and then, in a general sense, indicate the areas that may need improvement. Also may I suggest that our review not include all instances in one write-up, but merely make note of them. If Pastor requests any further interaction or if included, only state each instance briefly. .

To the pastor:

The board member is pastor's advisor, helper, and prayer partner. In this position he is a loyal supporter to the pastor, assisting him to fulfill the vision and goals God has given him for the local church. The pastor is the chairman and a voting member of the church boards.

To each other:

Board members are a team, working together within the scope of their assignment with a view for achieving the successful advancement of the church. Board members should seek to develop a close relationship through mutual prayer, worship and cooperative co-laboring with the pastor and his staff.

To the congregation:

Board members should promote goodwill in the congregation and should strengthen the people's confidence in their pastor and his leadership. The spiritual interest and welfare of the congregation are their concern and responsibility.

And then, a conclusion is made to the document that the pastor is God's gift to the church; and that the board members are the church's gift to the pastor.

These statements cause me to ask myself some questions regarding our relationship with our Pastor.

Right now, can we truthfully say that we, as a Board, are Pastor's advisors, helpers and prayer partners? Or to be even more direct, does Pastor consider us to be so? I think the question asked of us by a pastoral staff member was appropriate. "'How do you view your relationship with the board and the pastor?'"

The answer speaks clearly to the fact that we are not his advisors, that in a very real sense, we do not help him collectively as a board to minister to this body and that we are not his partners in prayer.

These are all questions that each of us individually should be asking ourselves and if the answer is no, then we need then to ask, why not?

The next statement says that the Board member is a loyal supporter of the pastor, assisting him to fulfill the visions and goals God has given him for the local church.

Brothers, it is my observation since being on the board that not only does the board not loyally support the Pastor, but on the contrary it seems to stand in direct opposition to him on a regular basis. I believe there are men at this table who have not even read some of the books we were asked to read, and yet stand ready to oppose anything concerning a proposal for our church.

As far as assisting him to fulfill the vision and goals God has given him, is this board even aware of what our pastor's goals and visions are? Possibly he is attempting to communicate that through his interest in the direction that he feels led to direct this particular church. I believe that the success and result of other successful ministries shows us the need for this church to get outside of these four walls. This is the focal point of several programs.

This statement also speaks of a close relationship through mutual prayer, worship, and cooperative co-laboring with the pastor and his staff. If we were meeting with the pastor and his staff on a regular basis for mutual prayer, worship and cooperation, and we had fewer closed-session meetings without the pastor present, we might spiritually see more eye-to-eye and find that we have similar goals and visions for this church body.

Please note an exception: If a pastor has been found or suspected of being involved in the practice of sinful acts, then there may be a need, at least in some extreme cases, to meet without him.

Further to the congregation:

It states that we should promote goodwill in the congregation and should strengthen the people's confidence in their pastor and his leadership. The spiritual interest and welfare of the congregation should be among (our) concerns and responsibilities. Over the past few months, the only promotion that has occurred has certainly not been the goodwill in the congregation resulting in the strengthening of the people's confidence in their pastor.

Unfortunately, much of the lack of goodwill has come directly from board members or former board members. This type of activity can only continue to block and frustrate any attempt for reconciliation and peace in our body. All of us must put bitterness, hurt, and anger to rest and trust God to lead us on to reach our community for Him.

The last statement in this document that we have adopted concludes by saying that the pastor is God's gift to the church and board members are the church's gift to the pastor.

I pondered this statement for a long time, considering my belief that God does indeed call a man to a position such as this, and considering also my belief that God brought pastor to us to shepherd this body. It made me ask, if we really do consider the pastor to be God's gift to us, and that we have the privilege of being the church's gift to pastor (to be his advisors, helpers and prayer partners). If this be true, then why is there a constant assertion that the board is his employer?

Instead of standing by pastor, looking for ways that we can assist him in fulfilling his vision for this church, it seems that in many ways there are a particular few that seem to always stand opposed to him.

I watched with excitement and joy last week as this church body and others joined hands enthusiastically to serve the Lord in outreach ministries.

Everywhere I looked, I saw tears of joy, smiles of happiness, and the Spirit of God moving as we all came together for one purpose, to lift up and exalt the Name of Jesus. I could not help but think how wonderful it would be to have that same unity, and that joy and peace enjoyed at a board level as well, we all witnessed what God could do when we come together in His Name.

Everyone is still talking about what happened during the summer months. The stories are still being told about what God did, people are excited and already asking about what we are going to do next. I believe that God is powerfully stirring the hearts of our people to make a difference for Him, to serve Him in a meaningful way. If we, as leadership, are not united in purpose; if we are not standing by pastor and his vision for a solution, then we can actually become part of the problem.

The Apostle Paul told the believers at Corinth, 'I appeal to you brothers, in the Name of our Lord Jesus Christ, that all of you agree with one another so that there may be no divisions among you and that you may be perfectly united in mind and thought." (1 Cor. 1: 10).

I appeal to each of you, my brothers that we need to agree with one another and with pastor, while speaking in love, taking issue only to fundamental doctrinal differences that may lead us astray, so there is no division among us so we are perfectly united in mind and thought.

The Introduction in the directive on church unity, says this:

> "'God's method by which the church of Jesus Christ has moved forward down through the centuries is that God selected a man to be the leader (the pastor) and then gave the leader men (deacons, elders and board members) who would serve as support to the leader and as fellow servants to the congregation.
>
> It is understood that God has always chosen to give the leadership the vision for the work of the Lord. For a pastor and board to work together for the enlargement of the Kingdom of God is a beautiful and uplifting experience."

As I reflect on all that I've just said, I acknowledge to you, my brothers, that I really do love my pastor. He has personally counseled me through the years in the midst of personal turmoil and family issues that I could not have handled by myself. He has spoken the truth of God's Word from the pulpit directly to me in more instances than I can remember, encouraging me to walk uprightly in the Lord. He has encouraged me in a positive way to pursue full-time ministry when I had doubts that I could do it at all.

I further acknowledge to you all that I really do love this church. At a time in our lives when we needed stability and building up, we walked through the doors of the church and never looked back. This church has given us love and training and peace. I know you all share my love for this church body and are driven by a desire to see God move and minister to our congregation.

I also acknowledge my love for each one of you. There is nothing that would cause me more unhappiness than to hurt any of you in any way, or to cause further strife and division among us who sit at this table. Yet there is nothing more I would rather do than for us to become perfectly united in mind and thought. We may have to swallow some pride, overcome some anger, forgive some hurt, forget some words or actions that were expressed, but is that not what we are called to do? If we're to love our neighbor as ourselves, where does that put our brother in Christ? Can we not work hard at putting away strife and divisions so that we can in every respect be of one accord?

Paul tells us to "put on the full armor of God, so that when the day of evil comes, you may be able to stand your ground, and after you have done everything, to stand

Let's stand together in unity with each other and with our Pastor and not allow the devil to again make a spectacle of us to the world.

My Thoughts

What a powerful exhortation from one who was there during the conflict, and dealt in such a Godly way to find solutions.

As I pondered this and previous letters, I thought about the church at Corinth. The apostle refers to a particular subject involving taking our brethren to court, and why it is a problem to the body of Christ. Teaching that it is a shame for the leadership to go before unbelievers to solve the problems that should be solved among the leadership themselves.

1 Cor 6:1-8 (NIV)

1 If any of you has a dispute with another, dare he take it before the ungodly for judgment instead of before the saints? 2 Do you not know that the saints will judge the world? And if you are to judge the world, are you not competent to judge trivial cases? 3 Do you not know that we will judge angels? How much more the things of this life! 4 Therefore, if you have disputes about such matters, appoint as judges even men of little account in the church!   5 I say this to shame you. Is it possible that there is nobody among you wise enough to judge a dispute between believers? 6 But instead, one brother goes to law against another — and this in front of unbelievers! 7 The very fact that you have lawsuits among you means you have been completely defeated already. Why not rather be wronged? Why not rather be cheated? 8 Instead, you yourselves cheat and do wrong, and you do this to your brothers.

Is your heart as heavy as mine when seeing or hearing about a church split?   Or even worse, to read of fighting at the altars of some churches, over who is, or is not, a voting member?

How about the deacon in Texas who was accused of bringing his gun to a board meeting and shooting one of the other board members during their meeting?

How about the fight they had at the altar of a church in Southern California. What a testimony to the unsaved when the police had to be called to intervene between board members arguing and fighting over who was in charge.

Then there was the crisis that was reported to have happened in Illinois, when the Sheriff's Deputies had to be called to stand at each entrance to the church facility to check for membership cards, and if necessary arrest anyone who tried to attend the business meeting if they could not prove they were members. I believe that ended up in litigation that ended up in a trial in court.

Could it be possible that when some are so focused on winning, they no longer care – by not caring they open themselves up to be used by the enemy just as Peter did in Matthew 16:22-23.

> Matt 16:24 (NIV) 24 Then Jesus said to his disciples, "If anyone would come after me, he must deny himself and take up his cross and follow me.

Have you ever heard the old song? "Must Jesus Bear the Cross Alone"

> And all the world go free,
> No there's a cross for everyone
> And there's a cross for me

It's still true no matter how old it is!

A Final Letter from a Heart Broken Member

Are we seeking the mind of God or the mind of men? How significant that only five verses earlier Jesus declared that Peter had had a revelation from God.

We must not put so much confidence in our own righteousness that we fail to be mindful of the fact that the heart, if not transformed, is deceitful above all else, and is not only deceitful, but according to the word:

> Jer 17:9 (NIV) The heart is deceitful above all things and beyond cure. Who can understand it?

And in The Living Bible,

> 9 "The heart is the most deceitful thing there is and desperately wicked. No one can really know how bad it is!

The powerful minority is often responsible for igniting the flames of battle, but they are seldom the ones who litter the fields of the spiritually wounded and dying. It should be apparent that most new

Christians seek church membership as a means of living out their newfound faith within a community of like-minded believers.

How do we tell them, that in some cases, church members and non-members, including the leadership are anything but like-minded? Each Sunday morning homes are filled with men and women who have left the church because they were wounded in an unscrupulous battle.

Are we so consumed with the thought of victory that we throw integrity out the window?

Are we so consumed with our "cause" that we fail to see the effect it has on new believers?

How dare we recruit new members into our aberrant agendas and cause them to fall short of attaining God's abundance. Have we become so deluded by issues that we fail to see the damage being done?

Do we really think that we, as leaders, will not be held accountable for our actions?

What would happen to struggling members if we would examine our own hearts and confess our wrongdoing by humbling ourselves before men and God?

The Apostle Paul, in writing to the church at Corinth, exhorted them that when at the communion table, they were to judge themselves.

> 1 Cor 11:31 (KJV) For if we would judge ourselves, we should not be judged.

If we are to win souls to Christ, isn't it of utmost need that especially after salvation, we convince them that there is more to look forward to in church than wounded Christians. A church should not consist only of the survival of the fittest! That is, if we are to win others to the kingdom of God. All too often, the silence is broken by the high-pitched sound of a stray bullet. Soon a barrage of artillery consisting of unkind words explodes on the once still horizon.

My fears are confirmed. The battle rages on.

The apostle Paul was familiar with the hearts of those that, even with right motives, may come to odds with each other. He references the case of Euodia with Syntyche, and how the adversary can use even the most dedicated, to hinder the Lord's work by times of disagreement.

Phil 4:2-7 (NIV)

> 2 I plead with Euodia and I plead with Syntyche to agree with each other in the Lord. 3 Yes, and I ask you, loyal yokefellow, help these women who have contended at my side in the cause of the gospel, along with Clement and the rest of my fellow workers, whose names are in the book of life. 4 Rejoice in the Lord always. I will say it again: rejoice! 5 Let your gentleness be evident to all. The Lord is near. 6 Do not be anxious about anything, but in everything, by prayer and petition, with thanksgiving, present your requests to God. 7 And the peace of God, which transcends all understanding, will guard your hearts and your minds in Christ Jesus.

The apostle Paul continually reminds the churches and leadership of their responsibility to the Gospel to which they have been called.

Eph 2:12-3:1 (TLB)

> 12 Remember that in those days you were living utterly apart from Christ; you were enemies of God's children, and he had promised you no help. You were lost, without God, without hope. 13 But now you belong to Christ Jesus, and though you once were far away from God, now you have been brought very near to him because of what Jesus Christ has done for you with his blood. 14 For Christ Himself is our way of peace. He has made peace between us Jews and you Gentiles by making us all one family, breaking down the wall of contempt that used to separate us. 15 By his death he ended the angry resentment between us, caused by the Jewish laws that favored the Jews and excluded the Gentiles, for he died to annul that whole system of Jewish laws. Then he took the two groups that had been opposed to

each other and made them parts of Himself; thus he fused us together to become one new person, and at last there was peace. 16 As parts of the same body, our anger against each other has disappeared, for both of us have been reconciled to God. And so the feud ended at last at the cross. 17 And he has brought this Good News of peace to you Gentiles who were very far away from him, and to us Jews who were near. 18 Now all of us, whether Jews or Gentiles, may come to God the Father with the Holy Spirit's help because of what Christ has done for us. 19 Now you are no longer strangers to God and foreigners to heaven, but you are members of God's very own family, citizens of God's country, and you belong in God's household with every other Christian. 20 What a foundation you stand on now: the apostles and the prophets; and the cornerstone of the building is Jesus Christ himself! 21 We who believe are carefully joined together with Christ as parts of a beautiful, constantly growing temple for God. 22 And you also are joined with him and with each other by the Spirit and are part of this dwelling place of God.

We know from the scriptures that those in leadership capacities have the greatest responsibility for faithfulness and obedience.

There are references in the Old Testament that remind us of how God feels about the role of those in leadership. One corporation dealing with their own needs put an ad in the local paper looking for workers. They posted the following statement, we don't want applications, we want a commitment.

What follows here are the words of the OT prophet Jeremiah, it still sends a chill up and down my spine when I realize that I, except by his grace, could be among those about which Jeremiah speaks. If we allow the "law of double reference" to be used, it may even include some of us.

Jer 23:1-4 (NIV)

1 "woe to the shepherds who are destroying and scattering the sheep of my pasture!" declares the LORD. 2 Therefore

this is what the Lord, the God of Israel, says to the shepherds who tend my people: "Because you have scattered my flock and driven them away and have not bestowed care on them, I will bestow punishment on you for the evil you have done," declares the LORD. 3 "I myself will gather the remnant of my flock out of all the countries where I have driven them and will bring them back to their pasture, where they will be fruitful and increase in number. 4 I will place shepherds over them who will tend them, and they will no longer be afraid or terrified, nor will any be missing," declares the Lord.

Ezek 34:2-19 (NIV)

2 "Son of man, prophesy against the shepherds of Israel; prophesy and say to them: 'this is what the sovereign lord says: woe to the shepherds of Israel who only take care of themselves! Should not shepherds take care of the flock? 3 You eat the curds, clothe yourselves with the wool and slaughter the choice animals, but you do not take care of the flock. 4 You have not strengthened the weak or healed the sick or bound up the injured. You have not brought back the strays or searched for the lost. You have ruled them harshly and brutally. 5 So they were scattered because there was no shepherd, and when they were scattered they became food for all the wild animals. 6 My sheep wandered over all the mountains and on every high hill. They were scattered over the whole earth, and no one searched or looked for them. 7 "'Therefore, you shepherds , hear the word of the Lord: 8 as surely as I live, declares the sovereign Lord, because my flock lacks a shepherd and so has been plundered and has become food for all the wild animals, and because my shepherds did not search for my flock but cared for themselves rather than for my flock, 9 therefore, o shepherds , hear the word of the Lord: 10 this is what the sovereign Lord says: I am against the shepherds and will hold them accountable for my flock. I will remove them from tending the flock so that the shepherds can no longer feed themselves. I will rescue my flock from their mouths, and it

will no longer be food for them. 11 "'For this is what the sovereign Lord says: I myself will search for my sheep and look after them. 12 As a shepherd looks after his scattered flock when he is with them, so will I look after my sheep. I will rescue them from all the places where they were scattered on a day of clouds and darkness. 13 I will bring them out from the nations and gather them from the countries, and I will bring them into their own land. I will pasture them on the mountains of Israel, in the ravines and in all the settlements in the land. 14 I will tend them in a good pasture, and the mountain heights of Israel will be their grazing land. There they will lie down in good grazing land, and there they will feed in a rich pasture on the mountains of Israel. 15 I myself will tend my sheep and have them lie down, declares the sovereign Lord. 16 I will search for the lost and bring back the strays. I will bind up the injured and strengthen the weak, but the sleek and the strong I will destroy. I will shepherd the flock with justice. 17 "'As for you, my flock, this is what the sovereign Lord says: I will judge between one sheep and another, and between rams and goats. 18 Is it not enough for you to feed on the good pasture? Must you also trample the rest of your pasture with your feet? Is it not enough for you to drink clear water? Must you also muddy the rest with your feet? 19 Must my flock feed on what you have trampled and drink what you have muddied with your feet?

Cause and Effect

This final letter continues with the cause and effects of a church or para-church organization being in conflict.

A church initiated war based on the carnal and unsanctified nature of one or several, often becomes the author of confusion. It claims the innocent, and all too often the new converts, among its casualties.

At a mid-week business meeting, the uniformed, those not privy to closed-door meetings, stare absently into space while words, like bullets, are fired across the sanctuary under the guise of church related business.

Perhaps the art of war, as it sometimes exists in religious organizations, should be explained during the teaching of a membership class. But how do you really prepare newly converted believers for a possible war among the saints? Saints that they had assumed were born again? Certainly in the capacity of a leadership position, one would assume that they would have a Christ like attitude, right?

This is not unlike the war between Israel and Palestine. In this war, there were peace talks and cease-fires, but inevitably a lone sniper or a rebel group strikes out in anger and the violence and its consequences resume.

In one church, located in one of the Southern States near the center point of the east coast between Maine and Florida, they were constantly sharing the gospel. It was however, beginning to grow slowly. The pastor kept preaching the word, and by doing so, they were making progress spiritually and numerically.

In spite of their growth, as happens over a period of years, members of the congregation began looking (horizontally) at the things around them. As a result, some of the saints became dissatisfied with their pastor, not that it is always wrong to want a change, but situations that cause church strife are never a pleasant thing.

Let me take a moment or two here to make reference to a serious problem that often attends the latter years of a minister's life. It is a known fact that there are times when some pastors need to listen to those who have proven themselves faithful, that for spiritual reasons may suggest the need for a change.

Unfortunately, the older we get, the more difficult it is to find another pastorate. Many churches have no desire to hire ministers that are above the age of 55; there are even some that draw the line at 50.

Fearing the lack of income, combined with illnesses that often accompany aging in many cases, some pastors may not be seeking God's direction, and they may stay at a church far beyond the time they should have considered leaving. This attitude may persist, surrounded by a faithful few not wanting their long time pastor and friend to leave, even though the church may continually be decreasing in attendance and may have lost their burden for the souls of their community.

The reason they won't resign is evident when you hear them claiming that they built that church into what it is, and they have the right to enjoy the benefits of their labor. It is then clear their decision is not always God's will or direction.

Whenever a pastor or anyone else in leadership begins to take claim for God's work, serious circumstances often arise. We have no right to claim what is not ours to begin with.

While some may have been instrumental in building up the building and through their ministry experienced salvations and healings, it wasn't, isn't, nor should it be their church, owned and operated by them. While mom and pop ventures are often blessed in the beginning, in my candid opinion there will be a time when it must change, if there is ever to be a successful work at that location. Church leadership please take note.

There are things that the board and congregation can do to aid in the retirement of pastors that have been faithful to their trust and have little or no retirement program to depend on.

In one particular case there was a small group who were unaware of his needs, or if they were, they never discussed it with him. They did share that they needed a change.

Some of them were among the founders of that particular congregation. Several were in the position of control that we referred to earlier, and their opinion of needing a change was accepted by the naive and gullible, who joined them in their effort to remove the pastor. In this case, he was apparently dearly loved by a majority of the congregation and had little on which to retire. (Dangerous circumstances)

As sides formed, and the phones rang, the church membership became divided; some standing with the pastor, as will almost always happen, and the rest with those wanting a change. Some even started vicious gossip, or unsubstantiated rumors that could not even be verified.

While change is sometimes necessary, the method of approach to this decision needs to be maintained with the highest form of integrity and compassion within the bounds of good council.

Listen to Paul's exhortation to one of the churches of his day. Remember however, that the following verses outline the kind of person that should be supported.

Not all of those in leadership, including some pastors, have these qualities.

1 Thess 5:12-18 (TLB)

12 Dear brothers, honor the officers of your church who work hard among you and warn you against all that is wrong. (Notice the warning admonition) 13 Think highly of them and give them your wholehearted love because they are straining to help you. And remember, no quarreling among yourselves. (Why do you think he would insist that there be no quarreling?) 14 Dear brothers, warn those who are lazy, comfort those who are frightened, take tender care of those who are weak, and be patient with everyone. 15 see that no one pays back evil for evil, but always try to do good to each other and to everyone else. (Is it possible that he was dealing with those of us who have a real tendency to "get even"?) 16 Always be joyful. 17 Always keep on praying.

18 No matter what happens, always be thankful, for this is God's will for you who belong to Christ Jesus.

These very personal letters are but examples of the dozens of heart wrenching tomes I have read and had to respond to over my 50 plus years of ministry. Though there is nothing new under the sun, each letter tears at my heart as if it is the first one I have ever read. My prayer and my hope is that letters like these become a thing of the past...a sad and painful past never to be repeated.

Chapter 13

Heart of Stone; Heart of Flesh

We all need to have the experience of replacing our hearts of stone, with a heart of flesh.

Ezek 36:26-28 (NIV)

26 I will give you a new heart and put a new spirit in you; I will remove from you your heart of stone and give you a heart of flesh. 27 And I will put my Spirit in you and move you to follow my decrees and be careful to keep my laws. 27 And I will put my Spirit within you so that you will obey my laws and do whatever I command. 28 "'and you shall live in Israel, the land which I gave your fathers long ago. And you shall be my people, and I will be your God."

When it comes to personal agendas or bad attitudes just how destructive can those be? I don't believe there could be any count to the amount of people that no longer attend church or serve the Lord anywhere, because of what they saw and heard while visiting among the members and friends professing to be born again.

You are right, that should not deter them; but what if they are a new converts with little or no Biblical knowledge? What if they have been devastated by the actions of supposedly seasoned saints?

Have you ever witnessed a spiritual tsunami? The expression on the face of those facing a real one should be enough to convince us that we must avoid divisiveness and spiritual catastrophes, especially in our evangelical churches, and all others as well.

To some that have faithfully attended a church since they were saved; these areas of division and lack of unity have so inundated them that it's as if they had been the victims of a spiritual Tsunami. The divisiveness of our enemy is the key to many, many failures. Only God knows the destruction that has been caused in evangelical churches due to the unbridled spirits and uncontrolled tongues.

Uncontrolled negative attitudes have caused some to lose their desire to enter, attend, or become involved in any church again.

Human nature has not changed much. Without the benefit of a spiritual heart transplant, the nature of man has remained the same since the fall of Adam and Eve. In the book of Ezekiel, he explains what God intends to do for his people.

> Ezekiel 37:24 My servant David will be king over them, and they will all have one shepherd; and they will walk in My ordinances and keep My statutes and observe them. 25 They will live on the land that I gave to Jacob My servant, in which your fathers lived; and they will live on it, they, and their sons and their sons' sons, forever; and David My servant will be their prince forever. 26 I will make a covenant of peace with them; it will be an everlasting covenant with them. And I will place them and multiply them, and will set My sanctuary in their midst forever. 27 My dwelling place also will be with them; and I will be their God, and they will be My people. 28 And the nations will know that I am the Lord who sanctifies Israel, when My sanctuary is in their midst forever.

In one church to which I was appointed, there were several situations due to problems that had come to the attention of those responsible for the church. The result of these problems was several splits. I had to deal with some whose attitudes were ungodly, to say nothing of being totally out of control. Yet, they were the ones seeking to control the church body, while they were unable to control their own body. One must first of all be in control of their personal temple.

In the New Testament, Paul expresses his own personal conversion experience and what he expected from someone who is converted.

He records this:

> 2 Cor 5:17-18 (TLB)

> 17 When someone becomes a Christian, he becomes a brand new person inside. He is not the same anymore. A new life has begun! 18 All these new things are from God who

brought us back to himself through what Christ Jesus did. And God has given us the privilege of urging everyone to come into his favor and be reconciled to him.

It's All About Our Attitude

It is all about our dealing with those having a "bad attitude" ...observations from Chuck Swindoll

"The longer I live, the more I realize the impact of attitude on life. Attitude, to me, is more important than the facts, more important than the past, than education, than money, it is more important than circumstances, failures, or successes: it is even more important than what other people may think, say or do. It is more important than appearances, giftedness or skill. It will make or break a company...make or break a church, or even contribute to the breaking up of a home and family.

The remarkable thing is that we have a choice every day regarding the attitude we will embrace for that day. We cannot change our past....we cannot change the fact that people will act in a certain way. We cannot change the inevitable. The only thing we can do is to play on the one string we do have, convinced that life is 10 percent what happens to me and 90 percent how I react to it. And so it is with you and me, as much as some of us may hate to admit it, we are in charge of our attitudes!

Let me share with you an experience I had in trying to help one church with a severe internal leadership problem.

In this particular case it was a man (with an attitude) who had taken the place of the head usher. This was simply done by default; the previous head usher was now attending another church. The new head usher was not, to my knowledge, asked to serve in that capacity, but he felt that it was something he wanted to do. So he simply did it!

After several weeks of seeing the way he handled things as the head usher, I realized that he could turn more people away in one service, than the Lord could help me bring into the body in a month.

It was early one Sunday Morning, he and I both got to the church earlier than anyone else. I used that opportunity to speak with him about his attitude as head usher. I remember that I kind of pinched his cheek, and in somewhat of a humorous tone said, "Brother Ed, you have to smile once in a while." To which he quickly responded in anger, "Look pastor, I can smile when I want to and right now I don't want to; and if you don't get off my back I am going to blow my top."

I was so distressed by what he said that later I talked with the former board members. I asked them, "How long has he been coming to this church?" Someone answered that it had been about 17 years. My response was swift. "How can a man professing to having been filled with the Spirit for 17 years, still have that kind of attitude toward authority?"

Of course the answer I received was supposed to explain and excuse it all, "Oh, that's just brother Ed, he claims to be a Christian and a member here, but he's always been like that."

Over the years, I have been deeply impressed by some things I had not really noticed until several years ago. It has to do with the vertical and horizontal views of the choices we make. Throughout the scriptures beginning with the teachings of Jesus, we are directed to keep our focus on eternal things.

How about this verse? Paul mentions it many times, but especially refers to it in his epistle to the church at Corinth.

2 Cor 4:17-18 (KJV)

17 For our light affliction, which is but for a moment, worketh for us a far more exceeding and eternal weight of glory; 18 While we look not at the things which are seen, but at the things which are not seen: for the things which are seen are temporal; but the things which are not seen are eternal.

Chapter 14

A New Sensitivity

In our earthly body, we look at our circumstances only with our natural eyesight. In the Spirit world, we are encouraged to focus on the things above, using our spiritual insight.

Our conversion is more than just a thought in our heads, or thinking ourselves happy. As we read in Paul's letter to the Corinthians, 2 COR. 4:18, the revelation of John in the book of Revelation, we need to have our eyes anointed that we might see. Rev. 3:18

> 2 COR. 4:18 (KJV) 18 While we look not at the things which are seen, but at the things which are not seen: for the things which are seen are temporal; but the things which are not seen are eternal.

When we are saved, our vision should then be focused on the things above.

> COL 3:1-3 (NIV)
>
> 1 Since, then, you have been raised with Christ, set your hearts on things above, where Christ is seated at the right hand of God. 2 Set your minds on things above, not on earthly things.

In my humble opinion, what the apostle refers to as carnality, is when we turn from spiritually vertical way of looking at things and turn our attention to only focusing on things horizontally, through our natural, unconverted senses. It is my opinion; we are then becoming carnally minded.

UNCONVERTED	CONVERTED	CONVERTED
		↑
THE CARNAL MAN	THE SPIRITUAL MAN	
THE HUMAN MAN	CHRISTIAN	V
UNREGENERATED	REGENERATED	E
		R
SENSE OF SEEING	SENSE OF SEEING	T
SENSE OF HEARING	SENSE OF HEARING	I
SENSE OF SMELL	SENSE OF SMELL	C
SENSE OF TASTE	SENSE OF TASTE	L
SENSE OF TOUCH	SENSE OF TOUCH	E
		↑
HUMAN SENSITIVITY HORIZONTAL		SPIRITUALLY VERTICLE

As an illustration of human and divine thinking, look at the words that Jesus spoke to Peter regarding his statement that Jesus should not suffer or die on the cross. Here are the words of Jesus to Peter:

Matt 16:23 (TLB)

23 Jesus turned on Peter and said, "Get away from me, you Satan! You are a dangerous trap to me. You are thinking merely from a human point of view (horizontal vision); and not from God's (vertical vision)."

Jesus was referring to Peter looking at things horizontally or from the natural man's point of view, and not seeing the bigger picture, vertically through the anointed eyes of the Spirit.

We too, even as leaders, can sometimes be guilty of looking at things only using our natural vision, as well as hearing through unregenerated ears. Sometimes hearing but not really listening.

Rev 2:7 (KJV) He that hath an ear, let him hear what the Spirit saith unto the churches;

Verse 22. [Then Peter took him] According to Biblical commentators, this may mean "that he interrupted him, or that he took him aside, or that he took him by the hand as a friend."

The latter is probably the true meaning. Peter was strongly attached to him. He could not bear to think of Jesus' death. He expected, moreover, that he would be the triumphant Messiah.

In his ardor, and confidence, and strong attachment, he seized him by the hand as a friend, and said, "Be it far from thee." This phrase might have been translated, "God be merciful to thee; this shall not be unto thee." It expressed Peter's strong desire that it might not be. The word "rebuke" here means to admonish or to earnestly entreat, as in Luke 17:3. It does not mean that Peter assumed authority over Christ, but that he earnestly expressed his wish that it might not be so. However, even this was improper. He should have been submissive, and not have interfered.

Verse 23. [Get thee behind me, Satan] The word "Satan" literally means "AN ADVERSARY," or one who opposes us in the accomplishment of our designs. It is commonly applied to the devil as the opposer or adversary of man;

But there is no evidence that the Lord Jesus meant to apply this term to Peter, as signifying that he was Satan or the Devil, or that he used the term in anger. He may have used it in the general sense, which the word bore as an adversary or opposer; and the meaning may be, that such sentiments as Peter expressed then were opposed to him and his plans.

His interference was improper. Peter's views and feelings stood in the way of the accomplishment of the Savior's designs. There was, undoubtedly, a rebuke in this language, for the conduct of Peter was improper; but the idea which is commonly attached to it, and which, perhaps, our translation conveys, implies a more severe and harsh rebuke than the Saviour intended, and then the language which he used would express:

[Thou art an offence] That is, a stumbling-block. Your advice and wishes are in my way.

Jesus explains why He said what He said. It was a case of horizontal thinking, rather than having his mind and heart fixed on the reason He came. If Jesus had followed Peter's desire, he would have never fulfilled his destiny...the cross and the forgiveness of sin.

Peter, like so many of us, tended to look at the circumstances surrounding us, rather than focusing our spiritual eyesight on the things above, that which Paul spoke of in:

> 2 Cor 4:15-18 (NIV)
>
> 15 All this is for your benefit, so that the grace that is reaching more and more people may cause thanksgiving to overflow to the glory of God. 16 Therefore we do not lose heart. Though outwardly we are wasting away, yet inwardly we are being renewed day by day. 17 For our light and momentary troubles are achieving for us an eternal glory that far outweighs them all. 18 So we fix our eyes not on what is seen, but on what is unseen. What is seen is temporary, but what is unseen is eternal. (Note: "They were to come to pass; they didn't come to stay.")

Focusing on the things above is what I call a vertical view of the Sovereignty of God.

He continues. You think that those things should not be done which God wishes to be done. You judge of this matter as people do who are desirous of honor; and not as God, who sees it best that I should die, to promote the great interests of mankind.

We Are Encouraged to Avoid a Negative Spirit

In the 73 Psalm, the first couple of verses, Asaph makes it very clear as to why his feet were almost gone, and his steps had well neigh slipped. Listen with your heart to his own testimony.

138

Ps 73:2-3 (KJV)

2 But as for me, my feet were almost gone; my steps had well nigh slipped. Tell us Asaph, how could a man of your stature stumble so badly? 3 For I was envious at the foolish, when I saw the prosperity of the wicked (horizontal thinking).

While on our Christian journey, a lot depends on what we are focusing on. Some keep their eyes on the natural things involving the circumstances that surround us while on this earth, others to their spiritual credit, make it a practice to dwell on the spiritual things above.

Do you remember what the Apostle Paul had to say about this in his letter to the church at Philippi?

Phil 4:4-8 (TLB)

4 Always be full of joy in the Lord; I say it again, rejoice! 5 Let everyone see that you are unselfish and considerate in all you do. Remember that the Lord is coming soon. Would to God, we could all continually live in the attitude Paul describes in this next verse. I, and I am sure you do to, have to pray and read the Word daily, to even come close to what he is saying. 6 Don't worry about anything; instead, pray about everything; tell God your needs, and don't forget to thank him for his answers.

He does however, promise a real blessing if we experience what he writes in verse 6.

7 If you do this, you will experience God's peace, which is far more wonderful than the human mind can understand. His peace will keep your thoughts and your hearts quiet and at rest as you trust in Christ Jesus. 8 And now, brothers, as I close this letter, let me say this one more thing:

I have decided that what he suggests to do in his "one more thing," is most important, compared to what our adversary would like us to continually be thinking about.

He states a tremendous truth, as he continues here in verse eight; fix your thoughts on what is true and good and right. Think about things that are pure and lovely, dwell on the fine, good things in others. Think about all you can praise God for and be glad about.

Chapter 15

Beginning of the end:

Now I will endeavor to finish
what I had started to write at the beginning.

In many churches, especially some that have been established for years, there are almost always a group of people that I have termed vigilantes; they are usually a law unto themselves. You can't correct them, and you surely can't change them. It takes an act of the almighty to set that church free from the bondage they have imposed upon it, perhaps for years. They are always ready to defend against anything that might cause them to be removed, individually or collectively from their position of dominance or control. It is their piano, their pew, their friends, and they feel that they should be the ones that control the church. They are the guardians of everything involving "their" Pastor, "their" church services, and "their" facilities.

While many of the faithful have remained dedicated and have served the Lord for years, there are also, at least in some cases, "long time" church members who have often managed to hold on to their positions. They believe that due to their longevity, loyalty, and giving, they now have earned "HOMESTEDDERS RIGHTS." The church facilities, right down to the pew they sit in, really belong to them, at least in their opinion; because of their "faithfulness" both financially and by their attendance.

Here is an apt description of such a scenario.

It was approaching the time for this particular church to have their annual business meeting. It was also time for their pastor to be voted on for re-election or if not re-elected, to begin their search for another pastor.

Having no idea about what was to befall them, there was the usual anticipation of the congregation, especially among the new converts who were about to attend their very first business meeting. Of course, during this time and the time leading up to the election, there were mixed feelings among the congregation due to the opinions being expressed. In addition, there were incredulous feelings in the heart of the pastor as a result of things that he had been made aware. It seemed that these things always show up just before an election.

It so happened that several months before the business meeting, the 40 year old son of a church member moved back to their city. His mom had been praying for many years, and she believed his move to be an answer to prayer. He, his wife and family returned to get a fresh new start. At this same time, a very special evangelist from Texas was preaching a revival at the church he had attended as a child, so he decided that he and his family would attend the service.

Sure enough, in answer to the mother's prayers, and no doubt the prayers of others, he, his wife, and children all came to the Lord that evening.

What a joyous time, what a wonderful homecoming. His mom was euphoric and visibly blessed by their decision.

Thank the Lord! They were all converted sometime in September, several years ago. Soon after, they joined the church. The following January, they excitedly looked forward to attending their first business meeting as voting members.

But during this time the phones among the members and friends of that church were ringing off the hook; due to the fact that there was to be a pastoral election, a lot of things were being said regarding the pastoral election.

Those who wanted a change, especially in the pastoral position, began their whispering campaign. Although he was doing a good job, they would talk. They gossiped about anything that may add to the list of reasons why their present pastor should resign.

Unbeknownst to the new family, for which his mom and family had prayed so long, the controversy continued to escalate. The members of the two factions as usual, were having trouble distinguishing between what was fact and what was fiction.

The worse part of the whole thing was the attitude of many; those that had been "converted" years before and had now been in leadership in the church for a very long time. Were these not the same people that had prayed and wept with the new family the night that they were "born again?"

The night of the business meeting came, and in attendance was this couple attending a church business meeting for the first time. They were excited. It started off pretty spiritual, that is, they had a song and prayer; following that was a short time of praise and worship, then everything took a turn for the worse.

Oblivious to the attendance of the new converts, the vigilantes were already at work. It continued like it was a political caucus, of the unsaved. The accusations against the pastor and his wife, the criticisms of everything one could possibly think of.

Then, to the amazement of the new converts, they beheld the look on the face of one of the deacons; one who had prayed this "son" through to salvation on that wonderful night during the conversion of their family. He began to turn red with anger. Then the veins in his neck looked like they were going to explode! With a finger pointed at others, and with others joining in, he left no doubt in any one's mind that he and a few others wanted the pastor out of there.

That entire family was overwhelmed at what they were witnessing in the church in which they had just been saved. They watched those who lead the service, testify, and in general act and look like they were Christians, suddenly become insensitive to anything but what was on their agenda.

Finally, after watching and listening to what he thought was a meeting to bring glory to GOD, he motioned to his wife and family that it was time to leave. To my knowledge, they never entered another church. How many others are there in the world that have no desire to attend another church, especially to become involved in membership or leadership? What this family saw didn't just affect them; it infected them to the point where they lost all respect for Christianity.

If you are wondering who or what should change, please take note of the following:

You can say that he shouldn't feel that way, and you are right. But how are the new converts going to deal with the church war of wills? How can they avoid the spiritual deaths, wounds, and casualties of church conflicts?

According to 1 Cor. 8, and Rom. 14, shouldn't those of us in leadership take some of the responsibility for the failure of others if we are causing their loss?

What does the WORD say about causing others to stumble?

Rom 14:13 (TLB) 13 So don't criticize each other anymore. Try instead to live in such a way that you will never make your brother stumble by letting him see you doing something he thinks is wrong.

1 Cor 8:8-12 (NIV)

8 But food does not bring us near to God; we are no worse if we do not eat, and no better if we do. 9 Be careful, however, that the exercise of your freedom does not become a stumbling block to the weak. 10 For if anyone with a weak conscience sees you who have this knowledge eating in an idol's temple, won't he be emboldened to eat what has been sacrificed to idols? 11 So this weak brother, for whom Christ died, is destroyed by your knowledge. 12 When you sin against your brothers in this way and wound their weak conscience, you sin against Christ.

2 Cor 6:1-4 (TLB)

1 As God's partners, we beg you not to toss aside this marvelous message of God's great kindness. 2 For God says, "Your cry came to me at a favorable time, when the doors of welcome were wide open. I helped you on a day when salvation was being offered." Right now God is ready to welcome you. Today he is ready to save you. 3 We try to live in such a way that no one will ever be offended or kept back from finding the Lord by the way we act, so that no one can find fault with us and blame it on the Lord. 4 In fact, in everything we do we try to show that we are true

ministers of God. We patiently endure suffering and hardship and trouble of every kind.

Perhaps you felt that I was being a little hard on Christians. My answer is that no doubt I was. I was hard on those professing Christianity that have played the game of religion for years; they have used the church as their social, material, and financial home.

If we don't have a revival that brings us back again to experience biblical holiness, we will become servants to those that are coming against Christianity by the millions. Consider the following.

How many more splits will there be? How many more souls once won will become lost again as a result of a breakout of conflict within the church body? How many of those just holding on will suffer defeat at the hands of professing, but not possessing Christians? How many more professing Christians will be unwilling to change the way they act, what they say, or even what they do to be sensitive to the spiritual needs of others? Selah.

There is a sad story recorded in the book of Judges relating the rise of another generation that knew not the Lord or what He had done for Israel.

Judges 2:10-13 (KJV)

10 And also all that generation were gathered unto their fathers: and there arose another generation after them, which knew not the LORD, nor yet the works which he had done for Israel. 11 And the children of Israel did evil in the sight of the LORD, and served Balim: 12 And they forsook the LORD God of their fathers, which brought them out of the land of Egypt, and followed other gods, of the gods of the people that were round about them, and bowed themselves unto them, and provoked the LORD to anger. 13 And they forsook the LORD, and served Baal and Ashtaroth.

Judges 2:12-14 (TLB)

12 They abandoned Jehovah, the God loved and worshiped by their ancestors-the God who had brought them out of Egypt. Instead, they were worshiping and bowing low

before the idols of the neighboring nations. So the anger of the Lord flamed out against all Israel. 13 He left them to the mercy of their enemies, for they had departed from Jehovah and were worshiping Baal and the Ashtaroth idols. 14 They served Baal-gods; they deserted God, the God of their parents who had led them out of Egypt; they took up with other gods, gods of the peoples around them. They actually worshiped them! And oh, how they angered God as they worshiped god Baal and goddess Astarte!

Where does that leave you and me today? Are you, am I, part of another generation that has forsaken him and have begun to worship things that have no eternal values? Is our language, our thoughts, our desires, the same as the world's? Are we really no different than those who worship the gods of this world? Think about it with me.

Why not take a few minutes and review the scriptures that you have just read. or at least scanned in this book? Ask the Lord to show each of us where and how we might change; and through that change have the opportunity to minister to the needs of others.

While reading, take the time to make some notes, or establish a journal; putting your thoughts into writing. What should these scriptures and even the comments really mean to the professing child of God?

This is not about legalism, it's about sanctification, a Biblical truth taught all through the Old and New Testaments.

Some Final Thoughts

Do you find yourself in confusion due to statements that have been made by others? This may include those in leadership, things that they have said out of anger, malice, jealousy or the result of a Carnal Spirit. Here are some final thoughts from the word of God to help reinforce our thinking from previous chapters.

Ja 5:19, 20 (NKJV) Brethren, if any one among you wanders from the truth, and someone turns him back, let him know that he that turns a sinner from the error of his way will save a soul from death and cover a multitude of sins.

HEB. 6:4-8: J.B. Philips

4 When you find men that have been enlightened, who have experienced salvation and received the Holy Spirit, who have known the wholesome nourishment of the word of God and touched the spiritual resources of the eternal world and who then fall away, it proves impossible to make them repent as they did at first. For they are re-crucifying the son of God, and by their conduct, exposing Him to shame and contempt.

The Early "Church" has a Record in the Book of Acts

The early "church" has a record of its beginning in the Bible, more specifically in the book of Acts. We know that it contains the history of the beginning of his church, and includes both the good, which we all have learned to appreciate, and the bad that has always been. It still is in fact, the reason that Mr. Peterson, in his translation titled the "Message" refers to the church then and now as a "hospital."

Spiritually perfect people are not found there. The true ministry of his church is to and for those who recognize their spiritual illnesses, and the need of a Savior and deliverer. This healing of the soul and spirit comes only through and by the ministry of His word, and its application to the life in need. For this, we need the power of the Holy Spirit to meet the need of a Savior, the one who gave His life that we might have eternal life. Since no one is in this life perfect, the church is not for those that do not feel their need for salvation, but it is for all those making redemption from Adams sin, a priority in their lives.

Having our direction changed, beginning with conversion. That is by and through the power of the Holy Spirit, accepting Jesus Christ as the only way to heaven, having then passed from death unto Eternal life. Our Savior, Jesus Christ, from the beginning of His ministry, gave a benevolent call that may also be termed as a command. "Follow me and I will make you fishers of men".

His directive to follow him was then accompanied by his in-depth teaching regarding the dichotomy that he established, that is comprised of the constant comparisons He would continue to make, between the world system, (a horizontal view, looking at our circumstances through our natural eyes), and his church, (a vertical view, looking at the things we can't see with our natural eyesight, but with our anointed eyes by and through His Spirit).

In His final recorded prayer in John 17, just before His crucifixion, Jesus endeavors to finalize in the minds of his church body, the need to keep the world and his church in a proper prospective. His constant call was to separation, dedication and commitment, and it left little doubt of his desire for His church to become one with Him, to be involved in a separation of purpose and direction, and to be dedicated to His plan and purpose for coming to this earth. Keep in mind that in this life, the **devil all too often has a plot, but God always has a plan.**

Unity was and is not only his plan, but his central theme. He continually encouraged his followers to walk close to him and to keep their spiritually anointed eyesight vertically focused on things above. This is never been more obvious than when he expressed in that final prayer as recorded in the 17th chapter of John.

His desire for his church is made so very clear, and is constantly referred to during that prayer. His answer to the success of his Church was and is to be the separation between the horizontal direction of the world and vertical direction of His church. This was also known as the Doctrine of Sanctification. (Often confuse the teaching of the Doctrine of Sanctification by using the word legalism to define separation)

This means by definition in two parts, "separation from the world, and dedication to God."

Seventeen times, in the 17th, chapter of the Gospel of John, (in the KJV and more or less in other translations), he mentions the world system, and the need for his Church to keep their focus on him. This then would include unity through the anointing of his Holy Spirit. This he wanted to see accomplished through, and as a result of, his sinless birth, his vicarious death and his resurrection.

His message was always consistent with his purpose for coming; that was to redeem the world from the wages of sin, and to make heaven the destination for any and all who purpose to be there. This was part of his provision, through and by his shed blood, that through the individual's confession of the truth that we are all born in sin and shaped in iniquity, and yet, we may be redeemed from the penalties of sin and sanctified, or set apart by His truth, His word is truth. Although not yet being made perfect, but as the Apostle Paul expressed to the Church at Philippi, "having a desire, throughout this very short life, to become as much like Christ as is spiritually possible."

The Apostle Paul makes this point in his epistle to the church at Philippi by stating and having recorded it, (Phil.3) "Not that I have attained, but this one thing I do, forgetting the things that are behind, I press toward the mark for the prize of the high calling of God in Christ Jesus". (KJV)

As I referred to earlier in this book, his claim on us through his plan of redemption and his call to unquestioning obedience to his Word, which is referred to as the process of sanctification. It has been replaced not only by the religious world, but many professing members of his church, that are, in many places, now replacing or cancelling the teaching of sanctification, either through the lack of knowledge of his word, or by intentionally relieving themselves of conviction by the use of the word "legalism." There, at least in some cases, they can excuse themselves from anything that may be construed as disobedience to his Word.

When I have asked some, "what do you mean by the word legalism?" I find that many really don't know what they mean because they were just quoting someone else that didn't know themselves the meaning of what they were really trying to say. If they are referring to a call to righteousness, or sanctification that make extremely clear the difference between living a carnal life, and/or living by Christian principles, they are missing the teachings of Jesus completely, especially if we are to have the "mind of Christ."

Never has the need for unity within his church been more important. Our personal attitudes and integrity, combined with our desire to make him our reason for living and for even our existence as well, is really hard to hide, if one endeavors to live for him.

The Apostle Paul references this so beautifully in his letter to the Church at Rome.

Romans 12:1, 2 (KJV)

"I beseech you brethren, by the mercies of God, that you offer yourselves as living sacrifices, Holy and acceptable unto God which is your reasonable service." "And be not conformed to this world, (another translation states the meaning to be, 2 "don't let the world put you in its mold"), but be ye transformed by the renewing of your mind that ye might know what is that good, acceptable, and perfect will of God.'

Those of us that claim to be part of the body of Christ, with him as the head, need only to continue to make this life all about him. Include ourselves, as we, through his sovereignty and divinity fit into his plan and purpose and are brought into a direct and living relationship with him.

It is important to keep our spiritual balance when a church body experiences a time of conflict, especially in the area of control. It is evident that in any organization that preaches the true gospel of Jesus Christ, there will always be those that Paul referred to as carnal, vying for leadership recognition.

The Bible gives us many warnings about the diversity of personalities that were in the early church. Those whose woeful attitudes and dispositions thought more in the carnal or horizontal realms, rather than through the potential for seeing, not as man sees, but through His Spirit, seeing as He sees, not only from the beginning, but through to the end of time.

In all too many church organizations, there seems to be, to a lessor or greater extent, a constant battle by individuals or groups, wanting to be recognized and/or possessing a proclivity toward being given authority within a church or para-church organization. That would allow them the right to make subjective decisions (sometimes including their own agenda), regarding the present or future direction of the organization. This is often referred to as a power struggle. As a reader, you may have found that this attitude is no doubt a major problem in the secular field as well, perhaps even where you work.

The lack of unity is often experienced when the direction or vision of any Church or Para-Church organization, becomes the priority of an individual or group, without considering the cost of any scriptural violations.

When the committee's only vision is about ultimately growing in size and greater income, all too often unity is not considered. It is not included in the big picture that also includes his will, plan and purpose, part of which is to get his Church ready for the greatest of all days, the rapture of his church.

Unfortunately, when our vision is not to carry out the will of the Father, but primarily just having a larger congregation or a fiscally sound financial system, there is always a possibility of losing our original direction. In the estimation of many that have spent many, many years studying the teachings of Jesus, they may end up not being spiritually sound, but politically correct.

This then could result in some honest and well-meaning members and friends, who more often than not, become the victims of those leaders. Leaders who fail to take into consideration the spiritual level of those that may have been trying to honor them, and having finally succeeded, the church is now in conflict. After they recognize their failure by not prayerfully encouraging unity, they simply resign their position. Then they leave that church or Para-church organization and search for another church in which they can be in charge.

However, they do not consider the residual effect and the direct result of their aberrant attitude, being those whose wounded bodies become strewn across the battle field. They who "having been wounded, in the house of a friend" while wearing the same uniform, fighting the same enemy, have often become wounded in action. As a result, all too often they become AWOL from their church and from other members of the body of Christ. Some are so wounded by church conflict that they never return to a church again.

Since the Bible declares that no one is going to get by with anything unrighteous, we cannot or should not be defeated by those who even in the early church declared,

> "They left us, but they were never really with us. If they had been, they would have stuck it out with us, loyal to the end. In leaving, they showed their true colors, showed they never did belong." (1 John 2:19) (TMB)

Since we know that there have been and still are failures, even in leadership, we see a complete difference in the attitude and dedication of those in leadership who were involved in the building and maturation of His church from the beginning.

In the book of Acts, when Peter and John were confronted by the religious, as well as the political powers of that day, they were ultimately given the choice to either stop speaking in the name of Jesus, or go back to jail. I imagine that if Peter and John would have given the same answer today, they would have been considered politically incorrect.

They decided that being faithful to their Master teacher was more important to them, than the threats being made by those in leadership in the religious organizations known as the Scribes and the Pharisees.

Peter responded with the following statement. Acts 4:19

> "Whether it is right to obey God or man, judge ye, but we cannot help to speak what we have seen and what we have heard". (NAS)

In other words, they were going to answer to a higher authority, and regardless of the cost, they were going to be obedient to their heavenly calling.

Perhaps you already are aware that in the early years of this wonderful country of America, Bible colleges and training centers were being started that focused on Him. They soon became ubiquitous, and seem to continue to be on the rise everywhere.

But sadly, over time, the misguided need to be bigger, more financially secure, and more intelligent. By being well educated, they decided that they were going to widen the "Highway of Holiness" and kept widening the "Highway" enlarging the circle of "inclusion." Ultimately they would begin the move that would lead us away from the conservation of the purpose for which were and are still called.

As there became less and less bible taught, it then provided for the beginning of the trend to distance themselves from that which Jesus lived and taught. This included the cross, as Paul revealed what happened then and is still happening now, it "made the cross of none effect."

From then on, the Church drifted toward and became subjected to, the ambitions of others. Those who, by use of their financial ability and charming personalities, thought that they knew what was best for the future of bible schools and Christian Colleges, and the loss of the true teaching of Jesus, and the cross, ultimately over time, began to lose the vision and the purpose for which Jesus, the son of God, came.

However, what they thought was best for most, then resulted in many turning from a spiritual experience and relationship with our creator, to making higher education and college degrees, the epitome of the purpose of all religious teaching. Harvard, Yale and Cornell, were apparently among those, along with other well-known schools of "higher education," that, over these many years, have found themselves more involved in growth of academics than in the spiritual call or teachings of Jesus and His Word.

While it is the thought of some that, "The mind is a terrible thing to waste", not only is that true, but in addition we need to add that, not only are we to love our Lord with our mind, but also (personally) with our soul and spirit). These too are a terrible thing to waste.

It is my understanding that at one time, in these United States, in any religious organization that used the Bible as its text book, that the applicants that desired to teach at Christian oriented schools of higher education, must be a proven Christian, endeavoring to live by Christian principles, and they needed to have credentials supporting their dedication to Christ, to even attend or to teach at some of these Christian schools of higher education. Now, it seems in all too many cases, you can even be president or a professor/teacher in some religious institutions, and have most any belief about almost anything, (Atheism?).

How is it possible that we have been so removed academically from the teaching that our country was founded on, and still be part of their executive leadership and faculty? For those that study to show themselves approved unto God, and have studied the Bible, as the word of the Lord, I reaffirm in my own heart again, that "yesterday, today, and forever, He is still who He said He was, and His word is forever established in Heaven".

I thank the Lord that there are still those of us that believe that what He taught and why He taught it, is still the highest form of religious education that has been affecting our world since the Judea/ Christian teaching began.

When facing the difficulties that arise from a church in conflict, remember those, even religious leaders that opposed him and his teaching of righteousness, sanctification and holiness. Jesus taught then and through his word today that, speaking of those that reject his teaching, that "their eyes have they closed, and their ears have they covered, (Individually and collectively) lest they see with their eyes and hear with their ears, and be converted". "But blessed your eyes for they see, and your ears for they hear." (Jesus quoting Isa. 6)

As I have previously written, since he gave his life for our redemption, he is, or should be, the center and circumference of all that we believe and put our trust in. The words that he shared with those around him, and those that were spoken about him, some 2000 years ago, are still applicable today.

During any trials or conflicts, we must depend on his word, and not let anyone or anything take our faith from us. Hold on to the truth that, there is still, "none other name, given among men, whereby we must be saved, other than the name of Jesus."

In his letter to the church at Philippi, as well as to the Church at Rome, the apostle Paul made sure that we would remain aware of (Rom. 1:16). It states: "I am not ashamed of the Gospel of Christ and that it was and is the power of God unto salvation, to everyone who believeth."

He has assured us over and over again that the Gospel has never changed.

Prompting him later to declare, recorded in the Gospel of John, Chapter 5:29, "I can of mine own self do nothing." (KJV). What He accomplished was the result of the anointing that came in the form of a dove, and rested upon him. His Father then declaring from heaven that, "This is my beloved son, in whom I am well pleased."

Listen to his words to the Philippian Church, especially chapter 2, as it contains by theological definition, the Kenosis", or the self-emptying of Christ of his Godly prerogatives.

"He made Himself of no reputation, emptied himself, (of his Godly prerogatives) took on himself the form of a servant, and being fashioned as a man, he humbled himself and became obedient unto death, even the death of the Cross. Wherefore God hath highly exalted him, and given him a name that is above every name, that at the name of Jesus, every knee shall bow, and every tongue confess that he is Lord to the glory of God the Father".

I would remind us again, and to all that profess to part of the Body of Christ, that it is, in fact about him, and not about us, to God be the glory.

One of the most serious of truths that he taught was about the inability through the "eyes" of the world to "see" spiritual things. And the reality is that they had blinded themselves so they would not see the truth and be converted, He made sure that we understood that fact that "We could see and understand through His Spirit, the things of God that the natural man, could not, and more often than not, doesn't want to understand.

He wrote to the Church at Corinth about this very matter.

Paul wrote these words,

> "For the natural man understandeth not the things of God, neither can he know them, for they are spiritually discerned.
> 1 Cor. 2:14 (KJV)

You really have to be able to think vertically, not just horizontally, and not allow your focus to be just on your circumstances, but if we are going to understand the things of God, then our focus needs to remain on the things above, where we are told that moth and rust does not corrupt, or thieves break through and steal.

Peter's statement to Jesus telling him that he did not want him to die caused him to receive a rebuke based on what he did not understand. Jesus said, "You savor the things of man, not of God." In other words, you think only horizontally (like human men) rather than vertically, or "about the things of God."

Also, the Apostle Paul, in his letter to the Church at Corinth, gives us some insight regarding his God given ability, through his Spirit, to see spiritual things from a vertical prospective.

> Cor 4:18 While we look not at things that can be seen, (the temporal, or our immediate circumstances), but on things that cannot be seen. (Eternal values) For that we can see are temporal, but what we cannot see, have eternal values.

My Final Conclusion:

In the book of John, while John was reclining by leaning on the breast of Jesus, Peter noticed John's restful position and made a unique inquiry, he ask Jesus the question, "What about John, what is he going to do?"

To which Jesus replied,

> "Whether I decide to have him live until I return, what is that to thee? Follow thou me? (Jn. 21: 22) Wow, what an answer!

Conformed to His Image

The pressure's on Lord and I don't much like it,
This conforming to your image. You mean to say
I'm supposed to be like you? Willing to be a servant;
Loving without being loved; ministering without reward;
Laying down my life for those who don't want it anyway;
Dying, yet going on to love, not for myself but others?
Is this what it's all about, Lord?
It's what you did, isn't it? You turned the other cheek
and didn't answer back. You kept on sharing truth,
no matter what was said. And you shared it, in love,
with those who wished you dead.
You cared, and kept on caring
even when all your friends had fled.
You prayed and kept on praying,
even as you bled to death,
But that was you, Lord, that was your calling,
Oh! I see Lord, it's mine too,
If I am to be conformed to your image
and be like you!

Bunty Burke

Perhaps we need to pay a little more attention to the words," Follow thou me!"

I am a Soldier in God's Army

I am a soldier in the Army of my God.
The Lord Jesus Christ is my Commanding Officer.
The Holy Bible is my code of conduct.
Faith, Prayer, and the Word are my weapons of warfare.
I have been taught by the Holy Spirit,
Trained by experience, Tried by adversity and Tested by fire.
I am a volunteer in this Army
and I am enlisted for eternity
I will either retire in this Army at the rapture or die in this Army;
But I will not get out, sell out, be talked out or pushed out.
I am faithful, reliable, teachable and capable, dependable and determined.
If my God needs me, I am there. If He needs me in the Sunday school to teach children, in the youth or to Help with adults
Or even just to sit and learn He can use me because I am there
I am a soldier.
I am not a baby; I do not need to be pampered petted,
Pumped-up, picked up or pepped up.
I am a soldier.
No one has to call me, write me Remind me, visit me,
Entice me or even lure me. I am a soldier. I am not an idler. I am in place.
Praising His Holy name, and building His Kingdom.
I do not need to be cuddled, cradled, cared for, or catered to. I am committed.
I am a soldier.
I cannot have my feeling hurt bad enough to turn me around.
I cannot be discouraged enough to turn me aside.
And I cannot lose enough to cause me to quit.
When Jesus called me into His Army, I had nothing,
If I end up with nothing, I will still come out ahead.
I will win, for my God has and will continue to supply all my needs.
I am more than a conqueror. I will always triumph.
I can do all things through Christ my source of Strength everlasting.
Demons cannot defeat me, people cannot disillusion me,
weather cannot weary me, sickness cannot stop me,

battles cannot beat me, money cannot buy me,
governments cannot silence me, and hell cannot handle me.
I am a soldier.
Even death cannot destroy me. For when my Commander Calls me
from this battlefield,
He will promote me to Captain and then allow me to rule with Him.
I am a soldier in God's Army,
And I am marching claiming victory.
I will not give up, I will not turn around.
I am a soldier, marching Heaven bound.
Here I stand!

Will you stand with me? Guess what? If you've accepted Jesus Christ
as our Lord and Savior, You're already enlisted.

The big question is, what part of the service are you in?

- Active Duty: Serving the Lord faithfully, daily, on duty
  24-7 around the clock?

- Reserve Status: Serving only when called upon or twice a
  year, Easter and Christmas?

- Guard Status: Backing up the active duty group?

- A.W.O.L. Absent With Out the Lord

- M.I.A Missing In Action

They say AWOL is absent without leave,
But in this case are you absent without the Lord?
Why not give it some thought?

About the Author

Dr. H.S. Ryan was the International Executive Director of Church Enrichment Ministries, Inc.

For more than 33 years, Dr. H. S. Ryan served as the International Executive Director of *Church Enrichment Ministries*. He received his academic training at what is now *Valley Forge Bible College*, and his Doctor of Divinity degree from *Southern California Theological Seminary*. In addition, he earned a Masters Degree in Theology and a Doctor of Christian Education degree from *Vision International University*.

During his ministry, Dr. Ryan traveled nationally and internationally holding seminars, revivals, and camp meetings, as well as consulting with hundreds of pastors on issues of pastoral care and church growth. Further, Dr. Ryan has a comprehensive CD of resources for pastors and churches, specializing in Church administration.

The following booklets are included on the CD and available from the website:

- A Biblical View Of The Occult;
- A Biblical View of Homosexuality;
- A Biblical View of Idolatry;
- Seven Vulnerabilities of Evangelical Leadership.
- The importance of the Attitudes of Leadership personalities.
- The ability to communicate with church members and among church leadership families, or the reality of "What you heard is not what I said."
- He is who He said He was!
- Transitioning from horizontal (human reasoning) to vertical (spiritual) thinking! (Our human sense of seeing; sense of hearing; sense of tasting; sense of feeling; and sense of smell; being anointed by the Holy Spirit as part of our conversion from death unto life.

Dr. Ryan went home to be with the Lord in 2014. The ministry of CEM continues on through his wife, Pastor Wanda Ryan.

For more information, please contact Wanda at

Cell phone: 1-704-933-7752 or
E-mail us at CEM1442@gmail.com
P.O. Box 93
Kannapolis, NC 28082

"A ministry still endeavoring to make a difference"

through ministry, helps, and administrations.

CPSIA information can be obtained
at www.ICGtesting.com
Printed in the USA
FFOW02n0952281015
18098FF